FROM TH… …USE

Poems and Stories

from

Tyne & Esk Writers

edited by

Claire Askew

British Library Cataloguing in Publication Data:
a catalogue record for this publication
is available from the British Library

ISBN 978-1-871828-90-0

Typeset in 11pt Minion Pro at Haddington, Scotland

Edited by Claire Askew

Cover Design by Nick Askew

Printed by
West Port Print and Design, St Andrews

Contents

Introduction

It is a truth universally acknowledged that writing is a solitary – sometimes lonely – pursuit. The image many people conjure when they think 'writer,' is that of a lone figure, bent over a typewriter (or, if their particular stereotype has joined the 21st century, a laptop), agonising over their lines under a weak light. They might well be in a garret.

Often this stereotypical 'writer's life' is perpetuated – even coveted – by those who don't currently write, but think they might fancy it some day. It seems romantic: that idea of the lone genius whom no one else quite understands. I think in this era of instant news and social media, the garret with one candle, a typewriter, and no distractions does sound like an appealing place. But in fact, I'd argue that the garret is the enemy of writing success.

Something you really, really need in order to go places with your writing is community: a place to bounce your ideas around, get feedback, and put your work in front of readers. It's important to be able to celebrate and commiserate with other people who get what you're going through. Being a writer is hard, and as the world of publishing shifts and reinvents itself, it seems to be getting harder every day. While focussing on your craft is, of course, a very sensible idea, doing so in the echo chamber of your own personal garret – be it a spare room, or a holiday retreat – isn't going to help you as much as you think.

That's why organisations like Tyne & Esk Writers are so valuable. They provide that essential writing community that all good writers, in my opinion, need to draw on. Tyne & Esk Writers has – at the time of writing – eight creative writing groups across Mid- and East Lothian, and all of them provide a safe, democratic and volunteer-run space where all writers are welcomed, and where there's no such thing as a stupid question. It's been a privilege to work with and for these groups over the past year – to welcome new members, and to watch the various ways in which each group's writers have provided mutual support, encouragement, and camaraderie.

The positive effects of participation in this community can be seen in the brilliant work inside these pages. The vast majority of the writers here have already presented their poem or story to their writing group peers, and have had the opportunity to rework and polish that piece for inclusion in this anthology. I'm happy to say that this book showcases some of the very best poetry and fiction from all of the eight Tyne & Esk groups, and illustrates the rich variety of voices working within our organisation. There's 'Being the other,' a beguiling, sensual poem by Stella Hervey Birrell – an exciting, emerging voice from the Dalkeith group, who recently published her debut novel. Also from Dalkeith, Yvonne Dalziel writes poignantly about the complexities of female friendship in 'Going out with Alice.' At the Port Seton group, Neil McGowan is famous for his dark and twisty stories that venture into the very fringes of our known worlds, and 'Absolution' is a particularly gripping example.

This anthology includes work by some of Tyne & Esk's most prolific and successful writers. Shirley Muir – the author of 'Is that Davey?' and a North Berwick writer – has been the editor of the Tyne & Esk magazine, Scrivens, and was awarded the inaugural Crediton Prize for Short Fiction in 2015. Jules Riley's brilliant short story 'The Sale' is well-known at the Musselburgh group, and you can read more of his fiction in his recently-published collection, *The Man in the Sepia Photographs*. This book also contains works by brand new, up-and-coming young writers like Sarah McLean, who's 22 – her poem 'Ode to the Cliché' is testament to her versatility as a writer, since she's also about to complete a multi-layered crime novel that I anticipate will be a best-seller. I'm very pleased to be able to include Luke Townsley's 'The Greatest Stories' here, too – at 16, Luke is already delighting his peers at the Haddington group with extracts from a gritty urban graphic novel.

I wish I could single out every piece in the anthology for particular praise: every story and poem here is the work of a dedicated and accomplished writer. But the far more sensible thing to do would be to stop taking up valuable time and space, and allow you, the reader, to get on with the task that awaits you. I have no doubt that within these pages you will find something that moves you, something that inspires you, and plenty to make you think. This brilliant patchwork of creative writing is the result of a thriving artistic community at the height of its powers. If being a part of that sounds good to you, I hope you'll step out of the garret and join us – just visit tyne-esk-writers.com for more information!

Happy reading,

Claire Askew

Heart to Heart

Dianne Alexander

Day One

"Riley! Where's my coffee, and that report? If it's not here go down to the Coroner's office and get it. Green, Brown, Black, Grey, my office, now."

D.I. Mal Grimshaw hollered, his hand flapping back and forth impatiently, signalling his subordinates to hasten their pace. They obeyed tentatively, slyly jockeying for the position of being last one in and therefore the one closest to the escape route. Being in that room, and least of all with Grimshaw present, was never pleasant and always scary. Too bright, too stuffy, too cluttered, and you inevitably left feeling damaged and grubby.

"Close the door, boy." Grimshaw watched as the tall, hapless figure of Green closed the door, and took his seat. He wondered to himself how he had been able to achieve such success. His solve rate of felonies was equal to none in the region. He had quickly climbed the career ladder in the force, and all with these four stooges as subordinates holding him back!

"Right! What are your thoughts?"

"About what, Sir?" Black asked.

"What do you mean, what about? The suicides. Not that that's what they are, of course." Grimshaw replied.

"I just wondered what part of it we were meant to be thinking about Sir."

"All of it, you prat!" Grimshaw shook his head in frustration.

"With all due respect Sir," Grey boldly interrupted, "Black's right. What are we meant to think about any of it? We've all seen the reports, there's nothing to go on, no forensics, no suspicious extraneous DNA, and nothing useful from the coroner. Anything on this latest one?"

"None, none at all, same M.O. as all the others. I sent Riley for a forensics report, but I could stake my pension on there being nothing to go on. Suicide note detailing every sordid detail of every sordid felony he's ever committed. Tortured himself, then slit his own throat. So what do you think?"

"There's remorse fever going around, Sir." Brown dared to snigger. A bitingly sharp look from Grimshaw shrivelled it painfully in his throat before it fully began. Green, Black and Grey turned to look at him, unsure whether to express aspects of admiration, awe, or disbelief.

"So who's the chief suspect Sir?" asked Grey.

"At last! Someone has asked the right question. Who's the chief suspect? Well, that's it. There isn't one left, unless you lot can think of anyone?"

"What about Charlie Findlay?" Brown offered.

The shrivelling look punched him like a sharp right hook to the face.

"I was only trying to be helpful Sir."

"Well don't try, think. The guy's an invalid, or don't you remember he had a ruddy heart transplant six months ago? I visited him a few weeks after. Weak as a kitten he was, all wrapped up in blankets. Wouldn't be surprised to see his obituary in the National rags very soon."

"Yeah, but Sir, he could have got someone to do it. Recruited someone new." Brown said.

"He doesn't trust anyone outside his gang, and they're all gone. Trusted us only because he had to, and the money he paid us was enough to keep us quiet. The good news! Apart from these 'suicides' of Charlie's Devils and the odd villain, we have not had a serious felony in the past six months. So there is bound to be promotion, for me. How do you fancy calling me Super?" Grimshaw asked.

The three subordinates didn't dare give even sideward glances – just sat looking straight ahead and nodded carefully and slowly.

"Right! Back to business, search the reports again; these guys didn't just kill themselves. There's got to be something. You just haven't found it yet."

Day Two

"What do you mean Brown's gone?" asked Grimshaw.

"He's dead Sir," said Green.

"Dead, what do you mean dead?"

"I mean he is dead Sir. Suicide note; tortured, and then slit his throat."

"Suicide note! What did it say?"

"Brown wrote a full confession of every misdemeanour he'd carried out in the force."

"Everything?"

"Everything, Sir."

"Did he mention me? What happened to the note?" Grimshaw asked.

"No Sir he did not mention you, at least not by name. I took it Sir."

"Good lad. Did his wife see it?"

"No Sir. I don't think so. She was in shock. She'd phoned right away."

"Where is she now?"

"At home. P.C. Rose is with her, Sir."

"Did Brown's wife say how it happened?"

"She wasn't that coherent Sir. Just said when she woke up this morning, Brown was not in bed, she went down to see what was up, and found him, dead."

"That's all. She didn't hear anything? No screams, nothing?" asked Grimshaw

"Nothing, Sir."

"Give me that note."

Grimshaw took in and crumpled it into his pocket.

"Okay, go get Black and Grey, go back to his house and see what you can find. Keep an eye on those forensic fellows. Sneaky sods, the lot of them."

Day Three

"Are you trying to rile me Green? This is no time for jokes."

"I'm not Sir. It's true, Grey's gone, same way as Brown. When his wife woke up this morning he wasn't in bed so she went down to see what had happened, found him sprawled on the sofa, blood everywhere, throat cut, looked like he'd gone ten rounds with the Klitscho brothers."

"Was there a note?"

"Yes Sir."

"Don't tell me, just like Brown's."

"No Sir. Worse, it described every detail of what we did to D.I. Alistair White. How we lured him to that parking lot, then watched as Charlie Findlay's gang beat the living daylights out of him."

Grimshaw interrupted: "Did it also say we called an ambulance and told Charlie to lay off before they killed him. It wasn't our fault he died on the way. I warned Charlie to just rough him up a bit to scare him and show him his place. I even offered Alistair a fair share in our enterprise. If we'd left him alone he would have had us locked up with all the low life criminals. He got what he deserved. And Grey, Grey was always a nasty little snivelling b***ard. Should have known never to trust him."

"I got the note Sir. No one saw it."

"Good, hand it over." Grimshaw took it, and – risking setting off the fire alarm and sprinklers – burned and crumpled it to grey ash in the metal waste bin.

Day Four

"What do you want, Riley? Snooping around as usual? I don't trust you." Grimshaw said.

"Green is dead." Riley said.

"You'd better not be fooling with me?'

"I was called out last night to go round to his house, and make the reports. I thought you might want his suicide note. Might also want to promote me to D.S., if you know what I mean?"

"Should I?"

"Oh, I think you should. Don't you?" Riley asked.

"Good-bye Riley, close the door on your way out." Grimshaw watched as he closed the door then lifted the phone. "Black, Riley needs the frighteners put on. See to it soon as. Oh, and my office NOW! Green's dead."

Night Four

"You're riling me Riley. How can Black be dead? He was built like a f***ing ox. My best man."

"He is just dead Sir. Just like all your other men. I'd be scared if I were you Sir. You know, no one left but you."

"Are you threatening me Riley? You are walking a very tight, narrow line. Did you do anything to Black?"

"No Sir, last I saw of him was outside your office yesterday. Said he wanted a word with me, then he left the building – he left the building, that was it."

"Did Black leave a suicide note?"

"Yes Sir, just like all the others."

Grimshaw thrummed the table. "Did you read it?'

Riley was getting scared now. Something weird was going on, people were dying all over the place. He wanted out of the room, to get himself away from any contagion that may be lurking.

"Perhaps just a peek."

"So yes, you read it. Have you got any of the Coroner's reports I told you to get?"

Riley was riled himself now, his heart was beating fast. "I left Brown, Grey and Green's on your desk." Riley took an urgent but tentative step towards Grimshaw's desk to find them. Grimshaw put up his hand in a stop gesture. "You don't touch anything on my desk, ever. Have you ever touched my desk? Read anything from it. You're a lying, spying wee toad Riley, never liked you never trusted you. You are out of here. Don't care what they do with you, but you are not to come within ten meters of my office, *capisce*?"

A wave of near relief flooded Riley's heart. He was not out of the office yet, but once he was he was free he need never, indeed should never, ever go in there again.

"Yes, yes Sir, absolutely Sir."

"Send Rose in." Riley turned towards the door sighing in relief.

"Riley!" Riley stopped; a shudder ran cold down his spine. He turned. "Yes, Sir?"

"The note."

"Yes, Sir. Here it is Sir."

Grimshaw snatched it from his hand. "GO!"

Riley jumped a full foot of the ground and ran from the room, dampness appearing at his crotch.

Grimshaw ripped apart the suicide note, not daring to look at what lies might be written about him on it. He emptied the bin on the floor, dropped the torn shreds into it, then set them on fire. Satisfied he had rid himself of evidence he sat down to think.

Day Five

Grimshaw sat on the sofa, sweat oozing from his pores and forming droplets. The droplets grew in size until their weight dragged them down his face, mingling with the tears and mucus that ran freely from his eyes and nose, and formed runnels that dripped from his chin onto the paper that quivered between his fingers. The salty liquid dissolved the ink, smearing the words, and turned the fluid black. But the words remained. His hand had written the words, but the words were not his. He was no longer in control of his own body. He had realised this soon after he was awoken.

Charlie Findlay, alleged invalid and head of the notorious criminal Findlay gang, now extinct, sat across from him, smiling and shaking his head.

"You know what this means, don't you? It's too late for remorse, Grimshaw. The Brothers Grim have fallen and now it's your turn. Come on, where's your bravado? No hard feelings, eh? Remember what you used to call me to make me look the fool? Here comes D.I. Alistair White, defender of the people and whiter than white. Couldn't solve a crime. But I *did* solve crimes, Grimshaw, and I did it right. I put proper felons behind bars."

Detective Inspector Grimshaw lifted his head and looked at the man through bleary, swollen eyes.

An expression of recognition passed over his face.

"You got it now, Grimshaw? Charlie Findlay got my heart the night you took me to hospital, beaten to death by his gang. Charlie knew whose heart he got as soon as the anaesthetic wore off, as he lay listening to it beat. But it was too late, there was no way back, at least not in this life.

"There was nothing he could do to fix it. Ironic don't you think?

"The stronger my heart got, the weaker he became, till all that remains of him is the body you see now, the rest is all me, Alastair White, and you were right – I am the defender of the people. Honest people. Now, Grimshaw, you know what you have to do."

Our Heroes

Mark Bateman

They volunteered to fight in the First World War,
in the trenches, in the blood and the gore,
hearing the wounded scream and artillery roar,
our heroes.

Battalions of friends were created,
to each other they were dedicated,
on the battlefield they were decimated,
our heroes.

In Belgium and France they fought the Hun,
they faced his rifle and machine gun,
they didn't flinch and they didn't run,
our heroes.

And in those fields of Belgium and France,
through thick barbed wire they had to advance,
they trusted to luck, but stood no chance,
our heroes.

Churchill said, *fight the Turks, we must*,
all the way along the Gallipoli isthmus,
we thought they'd have been home by Christmas,
our heroes.

In 1916 the Battle of the Somme,
through no-man's land they had to run,
there they were mown down one by one,
our heroes.

Even deep trenches weren't safe, alas,
as the wind brought phosgene or mustard gas,
our brave soldiers were cut down *en masse*,
our heroes.

But our brave boys didn't yield,
in the mud and glaur of Paschendaele's field,
they were our country's protecting shield,
our heroes.

1918 extinguished the burning embers,
it was all over on the 11th November,
and that's the date, when we will remember
our heroes.

At the Hairdresser's

Margaret Beck

"Pairs of knickers?"

"Well, how many do I take for an eighteen day holiday?"

"Lots, I imagine – put your head down a wee bit."

"Know what my friend says?"

"No, what?"

"Five pairs… and she's travelled everywhere."

"Is that right?"

"Oh aye, been everywhere – Abby Dabby, Manshu Pinchu, Benidorm – you name it, she's been there."

"Five pairs?"

"So she says."

"Five pairs, eighteen days – will I cut it a bit shorter here?"

"Aye, not too much – leave enough to cover my hearing aid."

"Five pairs? How does she manage?"

"Says it's easy: at night, wash the pair you've had on and wring it in a towel, then fold it in the bath mat and stamp up and down. Hang it somewhere."

"But the towel will be soaking wet!"

"Doesnae matter, you're in a different hotel every night."

"A bit more off your fringe?"

"Just a wee bit."

"Tell you what. I'd get a few of those packs of five in M&S, to be on the safe side. You can get them in black. How's that at the back?"

"Oh, that's lovely, thank you."

"Well, enjoy your holiday! See you later."

Being the Other

Stella Hervey Birrell

Feathered head, fur lined eye. Horn. Glittering sequin swathe.

Joy-keening, ground-shake stamping.
Released sound; clackating, whimpsnorting.

Nectar. Sweat-sour. Honey, sperm, menstrual fibre.

Perfume. Altering smoke. Foul-sweet breath. Deep-sweat, dripping.

Feathers. Fur. Bone. Soft shards. And skin, and skin, and skin.

Infatuation

Stuart Blair

is a breath-holding rollercoaster ride,
the anticipatory climb uphill;
to hang, as a cable car over space;
to stand, as a conquering mountaineer;
to wait, engine poised at its biting point,
self-determination hurtling down a chute.
Love is the slow trace on an ECG,
the walk round flower beds in a Botanics,
the trip to the zoo, a paddle in the sea,
a 2D image painted by romantics.
So long as man can breathe he'll sing of love
and like its rhymes, it's all a load of guff.

Full Moon

Rita Bradd

I am
She-Wolf summoned
by the golden moon
reflecting on ripening corn.

It's a solitary light luring me
and I glance over to see my grown cub
lurching at my flank,

our wellington boots exhale
with every step, wine spills
from our glasses, bleeds into the ageing dark,

soaks our fur till we are matted together
just as we were at the time of her birth
when our connection was split

and she grew tall in a blend of strong bone
magnificent pelt, gleaming fur, all united
by the hot melt of her grit.

Our throats vibrate,
tell our bond to the vault we echo round.
Inside, our path is clear.

We link arms, dogged as we raise the pace
reach the top of the hill, plunge into the moon-bath
lift up our faces, stretch open our jaws, push out

wild yelps, our howls
puncture the skin of silence
and we are carried across the hills

over valleys to the ocean
where we drop
drink up the ripple of the night
rise up in fullness.

Fault

Andy Broadfoot

David does not sleep, he does not talk; he does not call me dad. They say he's not normal – his schools, our neighbours, my family. Well I know that, I live with it. *It*, I live with *It*. I am his father; David is my son. I too know it's not normal to twirl in constant circles, to throw the full cup of juice from the table because it's not what he expected, to do the same thing with his plate because he's finished. It's empty and has no business hanging around. Not that I know any of this for certain. David doesn't say. He is eight and doesn't speak. It's not that he can't, he has all the apparatus for speech, it's just that he doesn't know how to say the words. Somehow, in becoming alive, bits of his mind became scrambled. My gorgeous, vulnerable, manic, autistic son's mind is in a jumble of disarray.

Watch David take a room down in a frenzy. The room is like an animal asleep, about to take its last breath. He will stand there, paused in the doorway, his eyes darting about, his breathing heavy, strange noises coming from within him – babbling incantations – building, and building. His eyes will so briefly meet mine, and then he'll tear the place apart. Finished, he'll sit in the mess, his mess, the guts of the animal, a primeval beast in the viscera of its kill.

The doctors, the specialists, recommended medication. They didn't say he's not normal, they said he isn't *neurotypical*. Neurotypicals don't realise that they have a label, that they too are not normal. Risperidone is what they suggested. There are some side effects, but what can be worse than this? It would calm him, let him focus and shut down the sensory overload. That's why he behaved this way; he couldn't filter out all those sounds and sights and smells that came at him from the world. All that incoherent babble. Dosage should decrease in time. Yes, there are counter indications, possible epilepsy, maybe some drooling, maybe a little shake, don't worry about the insomnia or constipation, he already has those. The shake too, come to think of it. The bottle says *do not allow children access to medicine.*

Each time, sated, David was terrified and shivering. I picked him up; held him hard. He saw my face and it was flayed from his scratching, his frustration, the blood no longer hidden beneath the surface. I thought back to a flight I took him on. He wanted to sit in a particular seat but the snippy hostess was frazzled and told him to just sit down. He nearly tore her face off. I could still hear her screams. I'm ashamed to say, I sometimes smiled about it. He ate his yoghurt in great gulps and ran into the garden.

His big brother was so tolerant, so patient that I neglected him. There are only two years between them, but the world of a difference. His dreams of David were his own; he didn't talk about them, not with me. James was playing with Stuart, the boy next door. David saw only the sand. I sensed trouble but didn't interfere. Specialists do not interfere, they *intervene.* Interfering is what obsessive parents do, leaving behind a mess for others better qualified to clear up. He ran across the garden, trampling everything and jumped into the sand, pushing Stuart out of the way, burying himself in the fine grains. James and Stuart looked at him with open mouths, then looked at me and walked away in silence. David was a frail, pale little boy with a narrow face and blue eyes, but he had the beating of me.

David was two when I took him to be tested. He didn't play or talk, he still wore nappies and he never looked at me directly. I could never look into his eyes and see him looking back. The paediatrician was a gentle good-humoured man and I sat with him watching David with all these wonderful children's toys – books, garages, train sets. The paediatrician placed a teddy bear on a seat and talked to David about it, how cute it was, how it liked to be cuddled, asked him what he wanted to call it. He trampled it underfoot, picked up a train from its track and pushed it off the edge of a table, over and over. The paediatrician looked at me grimly and explained that it was cause and effect. He needs predictability. David can't project his personality onto a teddy bear, or imagine the train as a real engine, but he can know that it will topple from the table like a stone and hit the floor every time.

It was a depressing dreary sun in that sky. The worst things were crawling through my mind. David's suffering was my fault. He was my fault. What if he had not been born, or if that match of DNA had never happened? Those are terrible things to contemplate, to unmake a child, to want a different one. I often dreamed he was talking to me and awoke feeling dirty as if I had sinned in my sleep. People asked me whether I would have any more children. They didn't realise it, but they always looked at David when they asked. I told them I'd had a vasectomy. They seemed relieved that I wouldn't bring any more like David into the world. I knew too that no relationship – no marriage, no friendship, no family – like those rooms he tore apart – could withstand his perpetual onslaught.

David ran in, hid behind a chair giggling wildly; chased by James: *Coming to get you, coming to get you.*

I wanted to see inside David's head, I tried to do it when he wasn't looking but he always ran away. I knew he felt examined, a specimen, but me, I saw nothing. How could I ever know him? Everything in his life was against him, as if it all rushed at him at once, like everything had to be subdued before he could interact with it. Often he came to me, needing squeezed. He pressed my skin, pinching it. I held him hard. Harder. It calmed him. They prescribed a weighted suit for him to wear, it hugged him harder and longer and tighter than I ever could. It was a better parent than me. He doesn't wear it and I am glad.

One summer I took him on to the Knockan Crag, a great uphill walk, no traffic, so I let go of his hand and let him run. He just trotted amiably beside me until we came to a steep rocky cliff and the Moine Thrust. I had stood reading the tourist information chiselled into a modern-day standing stone. It told me that the lower rock was younger than the upper rock, that the massive pressure of continental plates squeezing against each other caused a great rift, a fault, to form. David pulled away from me. He scrambled down the rock-face and began wedging himself into a tiny crack in the stone. He squirmed and wriggled himself into the space, sealing it with his frame, softening the rock's edges, making them one with his body. He was looking at me, laughing, his eyes sparkling, bliss radiating from his face. There he was, my son, moulded into this tender stone, this fissure, this womb, its great weight pressing down on him, his body spanning eons, bridging a geological history of five hundred million years.

I got a phone call from his school, they needed me to come and get him at once, his pariah parent. If I saw David coming towards me in the corridor, in the street, if he sat beside me in a café chewing his food, spitting it out, chewing it again, I would run. I would go the other way; I would not make his problems, his parents' problems, my own. As I approached his classroom, I heard David's sounds, his screams. I stood in the doorway looking through the glass panel. I felt ashamed. David was on the floor, the teacher sitting on top of him, her bare arms bleeding, my son's pale face looking up at me. I saw him and stayed rooted to the spot. He was broken, helpless, subdued, and I was betraying him.

Soon after that, David started hitting himself. I was used to him pinching me, but the shock of him screaming, punching his own face, tore a deep hole in my psyche. I would carry him on my shoulders, people staring up at him, at his bruised cheeks, and across at me, seeing the face of a child beater. Then he stopped eating. His pale skin becoming sallow, his bruises scorched; his eyes sunken back into his skull. After a week, he went into hospital.

The room was quiet, the hush interrupted intermittently by babies crying. There was a comforting hum of traffic outside. David sat on the bed picking at the sore developing in the corner of his mouth. His eyes darted around, as if he was trying to see the whole room at once, anxious in case one part changed while he was looking at another. His face was paler than white and drawn tight against his bones, purple splashes around his eyes. He looked at me, but there was no acknowledgement, no sign of recognition. I approached the bed like a rabbit might sniff the dead body of a fox. It was him, but not him, a replica from which the vital spark had been left out. The nurse came in bringing a sudden burst of activity and conversation. David squeezed his eyes tight shut, then threw himself down and began screaming.

The nurse needed me to help her take some blood and attach a drip. I just looked at her. She said they'd tried it before and she'd rather not put her staff through it again. They hoped that maybe, as his father, I'd be able to keep him calm.

Two new nurses took David's arm while a doctor arranged blood sample bottles in a line, and attached a three-inch needle to a syringe. David did not take his eyes off the needle. His breathing quickened as it came closer, growing louder while his fingers whitened. He struggled and I gripped his arm tighter. A terrible high-pitched scream erupted from his cracked lips. The bruises on his face were livid and hot.

We all fought to keep him still. A nurse and doctor pulled his arm straight and splinted it open. The nurse inserted the needle into a vein. David squirmed free yanked the needle from his arm, hurling the vial across the room. It hit the wall and smashed, splattering blood everywhere. Then he relaxed.

Later he sat quietly on the bed, rhythmically dipping his finger into his mouth and wiping the saliva onto his clothes. He absently played with his top lip, rolling it and then pushing it up to press against his nose. The doctor examined his chest, his ears. Without warning, my son closed his eyes, lay down and fell asleep.

The nurse asked me to stay.

Stay? I'm here for life.

I sat in a moulded plastic chair, unable to get comfortable, listening to the raucous cackle of the magpies outside. The open windows were streaked with rain. I examined the back of my bloody hand and wondered what came next.

David is awake now, lethargic and spent, but definitely awake. He is all too aware of me sitting here in my crumpled clothes like some carrion crow unwilling to leave its prey. He is looking at me and I am remembering the David-shaped space left in that stone rift, that fault in the earth spanning eons of time, knowing I would give anything to get him back.

Ballad of Border Rail

Elspeth Brown

A train rumbles down the Border Rail,
it's a trial run, oh don't let it fail!
Madge Elliot hears it, a distant sound,
a tremor pulsating deep in the ground.
Her battle is won, her hope is fulfilled,
the line will be opening, just as she willed.
The trains will be thundering down the track.
Aye, Madge was thrawn and never looked back.

Yet the battle seemed lost in sixty nine,
just as it was for the Paddy line,
its route through the Stewartry taken away
with its halts on the hills where woodmen stay;
the line to Stanraer and the Ireland boat,
the winding way home disappeared as a route.
The Borders and Galloway lost their line,
but Madge Elliot was thrawn and she never gave in.

Madge Elliot stood against Beeching's axe
though he chopped, she didn't stop in her tracks.
She wrote a petition for Borderers to sign,
and give to Harold Wilson at Number Ten,
she marched to the door, with piper as guide,
David Steel and her son were there at her side.
Harsh was the answer, the axe would fall.
The Waverley line had hit a brick wall.

Still Madge was thrawn and drummed up support,
strong as an engine, they stayed on the route.
She bided her time, was watchful and smart,
with her hopes always close to her family's heart.
Beside her *Campaigners for Borders Rail,*

if they spoke with one voice they would not fail.
At last work began on the border line,
and soon Madge knew things would turn out fine.
Some new stations and all new track,
once started the project never looked back.
Madge was invited to Waverley station
surrounded by many friends and relations.
An engine, Madge Elliot MBE,
was named for her which is spot on, all agree
Madge kept a straight line, she was sure they could win.
They were thrawn, they were thrawn, and they never gave in.

System Been Shut Down . . .

Ford Bull

System been shut down for maintenance for the last 10 minutes – superglitch in the base server. Starting to think its dead 'til end of the working day, same as last week. Get bored easily; the devil makes work for idle hands.

Knowledge of programming obviously lends itself well to the lost art of hacking. Like many good things, you run a higher risk of ruining it if you strictly adhere to pre-established rules. If you are hacking following a how-to, bullet-point list blog post, you are probably hacking for all the wrong reasons. To be masterful / untraceable requires a learnt flick of the wrist, certain human spontaneity that the algorithm AI and bot-nets are unable to detect.

It probably goes without saying, don't use the work computer! By all means use them as an accent point, *never* as prime interface. With deck comps so cheap these days, there is no excuse to make this mistake.

Don't fit into their set profile – bend their expectations.

1

Generate encrypted volume using LifeCrypt.xT.3, a program *I* developed. Get it on shareware. So light the system won't even feel it being installed.

Install MaskNuit – this is actually a LifeCorp program used for incognito data collection/spying. If you disable its desire to link up to its mother server, it can be a useful tool for keeping you off the radar. Reuse their tools against them.

2

For peace of mind, I suggest building your own Cantenna. Luckily there are always lots of discarded energy drinks cans left in recycling bins. Quick clean under bathroom taps, some careful cutting and you've got yourself a remote antenna. Most office workers won't even RecogniZe it as anything other than junk!

It's fun to use LifeCrypt.xT.3 and its natural counterpart LifeCrypt.xY.0 in tandem. Hit them with a double whammy so to speak. Tread cautious ; the programs tend to get wave tangled if you wield them too close to each other. Find a suitable balance and run with it. And by god I mean run.

Having a firm understanding of your own OS is essential. This is how they catch you out – chase you back to your own system and rip the mask off. If you don't know how to manipulate CMNDprompt, Active air, KebezPower and ShellPro, you have no chance.

3

Find sub-domains of interest. My interests lay with the data that's 'inaccessible' on the public server. The data behind the 'bright lights.' Constructing a list of interesting IPs/domains before you start is a clever idea. You can scratch them off the list as you go. If you're lazy, check services online that specialise in catching interestingly constructed streams. I am very wary of these services for one obvious reason – it can't be that easy.

Lazy is bad. If you're lazy and you feel the need to do something subversive, what's the point? Why put on jogging gear if you can't be bothered to run?

4

Always use fresh string.

No exceptions.

5

You may be tempted to use automated process bots to learn and repeat your process. I can see why its tempting – you could complete over 7000 individual loop circuit lookups in about 100 minute cycles using this process. Seems sound right? Don't be fooled. I was in a meeting where they revealed that they accommodate 'batch bot-hackers' as they are easier to spot in cyberspace, therefore prosecute in meatspace.

Like I just said. Don't be lazy.

6

Address has no authentication and isn't public? Tread with caution. If your results come back jumbled up or weird looking, its likely a dead end.

If the security package used is an outdated version, it can be more a hassle to crack than it's worth. If the address has absolutely no security measures – don't even bother. It's a trap.

7

Don't panic.

Sometimes the places you are trying to access need a creative way in. Don't be afraid to use a burner phone to pressure people for passwords.

91% of the time they will put you onto a bot. This is tricky as they aren't as sensitive to your tone of voice and will never feel affinity with you. You can trick them playing background ambient sound effects mixed with harmonising tones that can scramble their vocal tone receivers, usually enough to connect you to a human. Its curious how the bot can sound more vibrant and alive than the human.

It's much easier to hack a human than a machine. Same principles – be gentle but firm. People are trusting if you know what keywords to whisper. Do your research. Be pleasant, but don't forget to be assertive. If polite fails, sound like you're stressed and rushed, they will definitely identify with this.

Get the pass phrases you desire, so you can move further into the dungeon.

7.5

If you don't feel you have the social skills to pressure a co-worker via phone, there is an option B, provided the target has a custom programmed web app. These throwbacks to web3.0 are fertile ground for bugs. You can disguise yourself as a harmless error.

This route should never be done on autopilot. Don't fall into that trap. It takes more time to do this manually, but it allows you to be more confident in your actions.

8

The admin is almost always protected using /BackdoorLock/ or similar anti intruder programs. If you happen to get blocked this far into the process, it's a complex case of repeating the process using a different intruder program. Accommodate for the program's limitations next time.

9

Inside? It's safe to run the auto spotlight process. You may think it's crashed – it's not, it just takes a while and can't refresh its interface when it's working, better just letting it do its thing.

In the meantime it's a clever idea to change your time zone and location to throw potential trackers off the trail. Whatever you change these variables to, make sure you have a location set at least. Nomad users ping alarm bells all over the security switchboard.

If you're unimaginative thinking of locations to fake, you can randomly generate zombie locations using the same tools schools use to teach school kids. Cracking resource if you can be bothered to untangle your wavelengths. My suggestion is that you can be bothered.

If you find what you are looking for, or, there is nothing interesting to steal – move on. ASAP. The lack of interesting reading material can be a sign they have isolated you somewhere non-destructive. Pull out the cable and start again.

10

At its simplest, Hacking is just scanning and exploiting, with added espionage overtones. Never try any of this without the relevant mobile malware: the more up to date, the safer. Cover your own back, have fun, be creative and stay hungry. There is no right way, this method works well for myself.

I can't find any interesting looking data or patterns. Craving excitement I decide to trip a wire; just to see what happens.

* * *

On cue a deafening siren awakens people from their stasis. All wireless is put on emergency shut down. All data flow is severed. AUG interfaces are replaced with yellow and black warning stripes with white text saying "WARNING LOCK DOWN MODE SECURITY RISK PLEASE STAY CALM."

The sirens stop. A moment of silence passes, louder than the sirens. I can feel the wireless re-activating, invisible data frequencies washing over me. The AMPS in my body as they struggle to align to the backup signal. I've had slow re-connectivity issues for a while, maybe since the ReTuning. Maybe even before that. I dunno.

I can 'see' the network but it won't pair to me. There is a second unnamed network here, just a blank space where its name should be. Its not UserGrid or AdminGrid. Some kind of spooky GhostGrid. It could be a strange backdoor left behind as a result of me playing with the system. Technically speaking, I should report this abnormality to the appropriate authorities.

I click connect, without really thinking.. No user name required. Password? I instinctively type something, An almost muscle memory reaction. •••••• six black dots. I click 'expose password.'

POIZON. In full fat block capitals. Hit enter. Somehow the password has been accepted. I ask myself how I knew that, I have no answer to my own enquiry. No time to get hung up on questions when there is a potential for boredom-destroying mischief.

The backdoor server has granted me access to the building's automated fixtures. I never thought they would keep all this on the one server. Fools. I wonder how much of the building I can control from here. Air-ducts? PA-system? I can do things without being seen.

SNAP! Just had a tidy idea. This is a Ghost server – perfect opportunity to create an *actual* ghost. Even if it's just a ghost in the system. That would definitely give my co-workers something interesting to talk about with each other. What a coincidence this is Halloween week.

I switch to the department reception camera feed. Every time the receptionist turns her back to the vents I fire a quick burst of cold air at her. I can see the panic in the way she trembles as she gestures for security. I can affect people without physically being there. The freedom is exhilarating, if not a little terrifying.

But hassling the poor receptionist was just a warm up. I crack my knuckles: time to get spooky.

I flush every toilet in the building at the same time. Flicker lights on and off like fairy lights. Turn the heating up to *full blast tropical meltdown* or down to *Arctic chilly Baltic.* I quick-sculpt a wee Pacman ghost wire frame and print it out from every 3D printer in the building. Reboot everyone's personal photo frames to that famous ghost photo from the 2020s. I play cheesy old horror movie sound effects through the PA system at eardrum-splitting decibel levels. I switch the waiting room and reception flat screens from 24hour live news to the horror channel.

It feels right. Almost like I should have been orchestrating this level of mischief long ago. Every new action, my logic tells me to be careful in case the boys upstairs in network security trace it back. Can't stop, its addictive: I like to think up weird things I could do next. So easy its irresistible.

Outside my cubicle: can hear screams from the hard copy printers, far side of the room, as they spew out a thousand copies of the 2020s ghost photo. People are already posting stuff about the ghost on the LifeChat server. Sure beats people talking about new stationery deliveries.

Warning klaxon plays for the second time today. I hastily log out from the ghost server. Oh… Christ… I've been logged in as 'Luke_Hussain_140268,' my personal work log in this whole time. Blood runs cold. It won't be hard to find me, I'm just downstairs! Oh no. No! What have I done? For all I know a platoon of storm troopers have been dispatched this very second to drag me down into the room with no windows. Legally murder me for high treason against the corporation. This cannot be good for my career.

Work up the courage to raise the blinds; expecting to see shelled up elite armed guards, drawing stun pistols from their holsters, bolting in formation to my workspace.

Nothing. Yet.

The Old Woman's Confession

Julia M. Carman

When I walked in late and dirty from the woods, Mother looked up from the rabbit she was skinning. "Where's your sister?" she asked. Then she asked again. And Father joined in, grabbing the poker. "You'll tell," he roared. The shouting got worse. I could've told them truth . . . I should've told them truth . . . but I mumbled "Witch."

Such a daft thing to say: there weren't no witches in our wood. And I thought I'd be shook more for the truth.

Instead the village cried witch – *Witch! Witch! Witch!* – as they marched to Spinster Walcott's. She was tried then hanged. My sister is still lost.

The World's Lament

Moira Cormack

The violin struck a plaintive air.
Its elemental cry rose upwards
cracking the surface of memory.
Seagulls soared in its wake screeching.

The world howled its lament;
startled, the clouds burst forth,
tears escaping to earth.
Gravity in full swing.

Sunlight rainbow-ed the drops as
they fell, splishing into puddles.
Pools of indigo spotted the ground in the north,
yellow in the east, the south, orange and west red.

Vibrant rivers gushed down to the oceans.
Glaciers of many hued ice crystals sparkled.
Feet dancing, splashing in the watery bounty
made the world a giant cement mixer

turning, churning, creating.
Crotchets waltzed over the sky,
quavers tremored the fabric of life,
music hummed its way into the forgotten corners.

Going Out with Alice

Yvonne Dalziel

After Alice was knocked off her bike on a country road, not wearing her helmet, her daughter asked me, "Marjory, as her oldest and dearest friend, would you take mum out and about if I persuade her to move to Edinburgh?" We looked at her mother, lying in her hospital bed, struggling for breath, her chest crushed and her mind disorientated. "Be delighted," I lied. The renewal of our friendship was one promise I didn't think I would need to honour. I was wrong.

Old friends are like sisters; you are fond of them but you don't necessarily want to spend your leisure time with them. She lived in the north, I lived in the south, and an odd phone call kept us friends without too much interaction. But the connections, akin to those of real sisters, are like bits of wool: they knit you together by the force of early experience and traumatic memories; losing that is a kind of bereavement.

We had met in a room with brown walls and green linoleum, in a Nurses' Home, waiting to be interviewed. I was in short crimplene and white high heels, fashionable among lower socio-economic country girls: Alice was in tweed with sensible, but stylish, court shoes. She was confident, and just assumed she'd be selected for training.

In the early days I bullied her a little, using the results of our IQ test to assert intellectual superiority in retaliation for my social inferiority. I would, during lectures, devise quizzes for her where her answers, according to me, were always the wrong ones. I half suspected at the time that she actually knew her answers were correct, but played along because she just didn't care.

The friendship only developed after she joined the Christian Fellowship with their 'no fun' rules, and was uncovered as a fraud when she threw a cigarette out of the window, setting fire to the garden. Matron, of course, thought Alice's confession was altruistically motivated to cover for one of the less socially equipped girls; she looked at me.

Despite her apparent naivety, Alice had an irritating way of being right; brushing aside opposing views to fall like autumn leaves. Nothing had changed. Her unshakeable sense of self put a strain on the revived friendship, and a football match wasn't quite city culture, but we had run out of other options: she sang loudly in the cinema and hummed in concert halls. The prospect of a football match thrilled her. "An exciting new experience," she said. And it was.

Strangely, Alice and I looked basically as we did fifty years ago; she still had short, straight, wispy hair while I was still average everything but without the high heels. The petite figure that attracted the more dashing members of the Student's Union was still petite. Alice always hooked the medics, and got invited to fashionable parties, while I managed to extract the chemistry students from the solid mass of flannels, tweed jackets and ties that ranged along the walls. They were the ones unable to dance, flirt, or generate any sexual chemistry; not that I bore grudges. We settled into our seats.

"Isn't this wonderful? Lovely families being together?" Her hyperbole made me grumpy.

"Just a football match," I muttered.

"Listen to that lovely singing," she trilled. But the joyful harmony soon ended as fans switched to a different sound: berating players for missed chances and unfair tackles. Alice was deeply offended. "This language is simply awful. I'll tell them to stop."

There was a fearlessness about her that allowed Alice to behave in ways that could be described either as assertive, or just lacking in consideration for others. "Alice, don't!" But too late; she had already turned around, small face tilted, to express her disapproval in her poshest voice.

"I don't particularly appreciate your language. Such foul words." Overcome with fear, I expected some retribution, a bottle on my head, a torrent of the unacceptable language; but none came.

"Sorry missus. No offense."

Alice wasn't finished. "Now, you look like very nice gentlemen," she said, and proceeded to distract them from goalmouth incidents with endless questions. But that same quirk of personality that allowed Alice to believe her view of the world was central, transferred itself to the fans and shifted the atmosphere from potential conflict into conviviality. I didn't engage, fearing the mood would change. At half-time she jumped the queue for pies while I cowered at the back, trying to avoid her.

"I just barged in," she wheezed. "Nobody minds an old lady getting served first, do they? No salad, but these are lovely chips." She paused for breath.

"Alice, you okay? You seem a bit puffed."

"Stop fussing, Marjory! Why is everything doom and gloom with you? You never enjoy anything."

I bristled.

Midway through the second half, after she'd had a nap, and the men behind had decided they actually wanted to watch the game, Alice was suddenly struggling for breath. The men behind took charge and there was mayhem as help arrived. Alice was hyperventilating as she was carried off, her voice muted and strained, "Imagine . . . being carried . . . my age . . . by young . . . man?"

I am once again in a hospital room discussing Alice with her daughter. The tubes, oxygen masks and breathing machines are now redundant as she looks at me over Alice's body. "A football match, Marjory, at your age? Really, all those people, so bad for mother. I thought you just did concerts and cinema."

"It wasn't my fault, Matron," echoed in my head.

Then, unexpectedly, the tears came. The regret at the embarrassment, the petty irritations, the unkindness of caring too much what other people thought. Alice, largely insensitive to criticism, used her sense of entitlement to get what she wanted, made friends, spread fun and joy, and was never aware of the impact she had on others.

Then relief mingled with loss; one old friend less. How they are going.

Bleak Law, Lammermuir Hills

Mike Davenport

Why did I wake at 5am whispering its name?
Perhaps it resonated with a dream of desolation:
alone in an empty land, all friends and family gone.

Bleak Law, not one of those clichéd mountains
of inspiration, hardly a separate hill;
a bump on the shoulder of Lammer Law.

I trudge there by Hopes Reservoir, the sky
suitably grey and the purple bloom has passed.
I ascend, soot on trousers from burned heather.

Stirred by a raw wind, the hill's name
occupies the air, spreads over all
the presences of these high places:

late autumn withered bracken; harsh staccato
call of grouse; a rusting cartridge case;
soaked rabbit corpse, bones protruding.

Jamie

Pat Dickson

I was not sorry when April 1982 arrived, and one of my pupils departed. Being Headmistress of a fairly large primary school was a challenge, and one I enjoyed. There was a diverse mix of children, from fishermen's sons and daughters who might appear in clothing which in no way resembled our uniform of grey shorts or skirts, grey pullovers, white shirts and red ties. These children were quick with their fists, and their language left a lot to be desired, but I liked them, tribes of Patersons, or Collins, or Dougals, who tended to all live down by the harbour. Then there were the mass of ordinary children from middle class homes, and at the other spectrum, came the children from wealthier families, whose children were destined to go on to fee paying schools in Edinburgh, or even boarding school. Jamie was one of these.

He started school aged five in 1975, and was as full of original sin as any child I had ever come across. He was small for his age, blonde, had twinkly blue eyes, and a smile that would melt butter. I'm sure his mother did her best and sent him to school as smartly dressed as his big brother, two years older and a model pupil, but by the time Jamie arrived in the classroom, his tie would be adrift, his shoes scuffed, and his knees scarred and muddy. He came to my attention on his very first day at school when I looked out of my window at morning playtime, and saw the whole school gazing upward at the roof. Curiosity got the better of me and I left the office and went down to the playground and looked up. There, on the flat roof, two storeys up, was the figure of a tiny boy doing a sort of step dance. My first instinct was to shout, "Get down here at once," but common sense prevailed, and I sent one of the older boys to fetch the janitor and a long ladder, "Immediately!" When the young culprit was brought to my room, he was utterly unrepentant of his crime.

"This is your very first morning at school," I said. "Do you think you've made a good start?"

"Oh yes!" he replied. "It was lovely up there. Have you been up?"

"Certainly not! It would not be seemly for a Headmistress to climb on the roof. And how did you get up there?"

"I climbed up the drainpipe. I'm a very good climber. But it wouldn't be easy with your skirt on. Maybe . . ."

"Enough! It is not permitted to climb on the roof. Do you understand that?"

"Well I do now. But nobody told me before. It's a shame you can't see it, you would like it up there."

I decided not to punish him, he was so tiny and so smiley, and it was his first day.

Some time later, I enquired of Miss Hunter, Head of the Infant School, and Jamie's teacher, how he was getting on.

"Oh, he's a complete rogue," she replied. "He entices the girls into the Wendy House, and then he kisses them. Unfortunately, they seem to like it."

"Keep a very close eye on that boy. He needs watching."

"When he attained Primary 2, at the ripe old age of six, he was marched to my office again. This time it was for breaking the glasses of one of our prefects, a big boy of eleven.

"Well, Jamie. What have you to say for yourself?"

"I didn't mean to break his glasses. He was being really mean to me and I hit his chin, hard, and his face sort of shoogled and his glasses fell off."

I found it very hard not to laugh, especially as the prefect was not one of our more successful appointments, a prig and a bit of a bully, but I had to do my duty.

"Jamie, I am going to telephone to your mother, and you will spend the rest of the day at home. I am very displeased with you. You can wait outside in the corridor until she arrives."

When Mrs Scott arrived, she apologised for Jamie. "He really is a very naughty boy, but there's one good thing about Jamie, he never tells a lie."

And that, I found out, was true. He would get into the most appalling scrapes, but always owned up. "It was me," he would say, with those blue eyes twinkling and that beguiling smile.

Terms pass by and years pass by, and now Jamie's big brother is our Head Boy, and his little sister turns out to be extremely clever and no problem at all. I wonder if it is the middle child syndrome that causes Jamie to be constantly in trouble. Every teacher he has had turns into a nervous wreck, not knowing what he's going to do next. There are frequent trips to our local A & E, necessitating stitches or worse, as his derring do attitude to life takes its toll. The nurses there have threatened to put up a plaque to him, as he's such a frequent visitor. Like his little sister, he's extremely clever, and I sometimes wonder if he will turn out to be a master criminal. When he reached the dizzy heights of Primary 7, he had a male teacher, and I hoped that he might help Jamie channel his activities into a more responsible form. My hope was in vain. Mr MacRae turned from a quiet but confident teacher into a gibbering mass of nerves. Jamie's final ploy was to unscrew all the cupboard doors in his classroom, so finely that they all stood in place until one was touched, then they all fell down with such a crash that all the classes on that floor assembled to see the carnage. That was the final straw. I had to suspend Jamie, and his parents decided to send him off to boarding school. I was not sorry.

Many years later, when I was well into my retirement, I was watching the evening news when a name made me sit up and listen. It was a report on a climbing accident on Mont Blanc, when a man called Jamie Scott had risked his own life to rescue two fellow climbers and had brought then to safety. There was a photo of a fair haired man with twinky blue eyes and a bewitching smile, wee Jamie.

Revenge

Lorna Dixon

The Harbour Master looked out of his window at the work going on below. His mind went back to the time four years ago when the wind had changed to the north east more quickly than forecast, and coincided with an unusually high tide. He had watched, helpless, as a tidal surge poured over the wall of the boat park, picking up the fragile dinghies and flinging them into the harbour, to smash on top of the moored craft and into the harbour walls. One of the boats that the sea had flung aside like a piece of driftwood was an old fishing yawl he'd inherited from his uncle. In his spare time he'd been refitting it. Although he was used to the power of the sea, somehow that night it had seemed as though an animal – growling, foaming at the mouth and bent on destruction – had broken loose from the rampaging horde of breakers, poured over the wall, then roared out through the harbour mouth to battle against the oncoming surf. He'd never forgiven it.

The new sea defences were looking good: a high curved wall of concrete surrounding the boat park, and a pile of giant boulders on the seaward side. There was only one small area to complete and then the sea would be tamed. His family had lived in the small seaside town for many years and the Harbour Master was well aware of the constantly changing coastline. Indeed, four centuries ago, part of the old Kirk on the headland had been washed away and the bones of the sleepers in the graveyard been cast up on the shore for years afterwards. As a child he'd been fascinated by the way new rocks suddenly appeared after an ebb tide had sucked back the sand. The little burn that ran across the beach had changed its course many times as the sea built up banks of pebbles to divert it. But now, for the watcher from the window, the battle with the sea had become personal. It had taken two years to persuade the powers that be to commit to building the new line of defence. Soon he was going to be in control.

It was getting dark and the workmen were packing up for the day. The foreman shouted up to the open window.

"We'll be finished this job tomorrow."

"Good, good. There's a high tide tomorrow afternoon, but there's only a light westerly forecast until late on."

"Fine, fine, low tide in the morning and we'll be done. Are you up for a pint in The Old Ship before home?"

"Aye, why not?"

The Old Ship Inn buzzed with warmth and chatter. Nobody noticed the clouds building and reddening to the east as the sun sank behind the islands. The lights along the beach road shivered gently on the damp sand as the sea prowled closer to the gap in the unfinished wall. Again and again it swelled up the rocks. Each time it retreated it gathered strength for another surge. The wind veered to the north-east, driving the cohorts of cloud ever nearer. Spears of rain were flung from the squall and a gust challenged the drooping flag on the harbour. It unfurled and stretched out inland to signal the joining of forces. Wind and sea conspired to take their revenge.

Fishing's Decline

Ian Donaldson

The fishing's past its sell-by date,
in Port Seton, at any rate.
The industry, once its main source of life,
routinely slashed by government's knife.
Quotas the bane of our local fleet –
"Too many boxes," the ministers bleat.

"We can't let you fish with such impunity."
But that doesn't help the local community.
Boats decommissioned, and men retired early,
catches monitored, but surely not fairly.
Fish is still plentiful to go around –
politicians ran us into the ground.

In happier days, the nets were fou',
the town's finances were healthy, too.
The local businesses and shops, they knew,
when fish was caught, the economy grew.
And now we fish wi' prawns and creels,
and keep the fish to feed the seals.

Family life was consumed by fishing –
fathers to sons, in quick succession,
uncles and brothers and friends alike –
a lifestyle long since taken a hike.
The prawns now the staple for our local boats
but quotas continue to get our goats!

The fishing characters no longer hold sway,
retired or deid or gone away.
Big John Heckle, his troosers torn
wi' nary a thought for the morn –
and 'Poultice' Dickson, covered in ile
– just the image makes you smile.

Catching great fish was aye in their dreams
especially in the bar o' the Wemyss,
wi Cookies, Little and Dick Lees,
we'll sadly see no more of these.
And Alec Stewart, wi' eyes shut tight,
always got home at the end of the night.

The local men, they liked the pubs,
like Port Seton Fisherman's Social Clubs.
And up from the harbour, in the early morning
Dod's back shop was always open.
A hard shift at sea made dry the mooth,
they stopped at Dod's to quench their drouth!

There's nae disgrace in fun and merriment,
because they've laboured to refreshment,
graftin away in the guts o the sea,
certainly appears fair dos to me!
Work hard, play hard, that was the rule –
a kind, but unforgiving school.

Unforgiving, in terms of banter –
fishermen's craic brought gales of laughter.
If anyone got too big for their boots,
the rest would surely sort them oot.
At sea the crews they braved the weather,
but when at hame, they drank thegither!

Though welcomed in, the 'incomers' knew
They couldny possibly be 'yin o ou.'
The fishing industry continues to wane,
the old place soon won't be the same.
"Still, it's progress," dissenters sigh,
but some still pine for times gone by.

Pure Physics

Paul Duffney

"When I moved back to Edinburgh I'd been doing work in quantum gravity but I couldn't see any useful way of extending it at the time, I was sort of at a dead end. I didn't know what I was going to do so first of all, in Edinburgh, in the summer of 1960, I was roped into the organisation of the first Scottish university summer school in physics at Newbattle Abbey College, before taking up the lectureship in October"

– Peter Higgs, from a BBC News article

1960! Yeah, that was the year Eddie Cochran got killed in the car crash down in Chippenham. I was inconsolable – I used to play 'Three Steps . . .' myself, on the guitar. It was the same year that I met the professor guy at Newbattle Abbey. Harmless fellow – a really quiet chap, he was.

The Vice Principal had stopped me on my way to unblock a bathroom sink in the college crypt. "Could I sort out a problem for the physics summer school people?"

"You can't risk a flood and that comes first," I said, "I will come up as soon as humanly possible."

I'm unclogging this drain and it's turning round in my head, "This is a team of brilliant minds, working on pure science: what do they want with me?" Turned out, it was to wire up their overhead projector. This was what was holding up their lecture – a plug!

So I got my screwdriver and had the projector wired in about one minute. The professor got the first slide up and I remember he put his hands together and gave me this wee dry nod. Nobody told me to go, by the way. So I thought I should hang around in case anything else might be needed and – to tell you the truth – I was quite intrigued to hear what pure physicists might talk about when they are let loose. The slide was a weird-looking diagram, like a film of soot with all kinds of spirals and lines scratched over it.

Well, you should have heard them quarrelling about something called 'quantum gravity' and then 'the strong force' and then it was 'the weak force'. I will tell you, the Black Bull on a Saturday night was nothing to this. Even so, I was taken aback by one young American boy who was shouting from the back. "There isn't a particle in the world that has a field like that!" He was bright red in the face and jabbing his finger at the professor. "There's no need for that!" I thought.

The professor was just looking at the floor and shaking his head. The angry boy was still at it – bawling something to do with 'quarks' being held together with 'gluons'. Then he screams out – and I'll never forget this – "Show me your math! Boson behaviour precludes your damn field conditions!" I was shocked; I felt quite sorry for the professor: you could see he was a shy man and he wasn't used to that kind of abuse. I was actually waiting for somebody to say something to the geezer. I was actually waiting for somebody to belt him one. But nobody gave a chirp.

Evidently, all these physicists were too much in awe of this belligerent guy. So I looked him in the eye – and he saw me looking – then I gave him the old *wha daur meddle wi' me?* stare. That quietened him down, but next there came a smile over his face and I knew what he was going to say.

"That's why you've got the janitor here – you need his muscle to back up your crazy boson theory!" That was enough for me. I turned to the professor and asked him: "With all due respect Prof., may I say something?" He didn't speak – just shrugged his shoulders. I turned round to the loudmouth and told him straight. "You're playing with fire, Son. If the professor has a boson theory, I think everybody in this room deserves to hear it. You're the black sheep, Pal. Maybe your bosons don't behave like that, but who's to say there isn't another style of boson somewhere that's in a different kind of field and does behave like that and maybe the professor will even explain it to you if you're nice."

That put his gas at a peep. All the other physicists were looking at me, with their jaws hitting their knees and I thought I'd better make my exit before it got ugly. When I was turning to go though, there was the professor, with his hands together again. This time he gave me a long nod. It definitely lasted longer than just a wee nod. In fact, it looked more like a bow. Down went his head and up again. He had a nice face, the professor. It was a very pleasant face and his eyes were darting about from side to side all the time. My ears were still ringing from all the shouting but, when I closed the door behind me, there wasn't another sound from that room.

"Well, that's got them all thinking," I said to myself.

The Sea Trout

Victoria Fletcher

She shimmered through the water
like a shining piece of steel.
No hook or eye would court her,
no tickler's hand would feel.

The silver dart rushed onward
to swim amongst the seal,
past rocks and moor and homeland,
no fisherman's easy meal.

Yester Beeches

Victoria Fletcher

I wander up Yester drive
where, neath the sky,
tall beeches strive
against each other
to reach most high,
and at their feet
leaves from countless years:
all colours, soft and deep.

A Musical Instrument

Moira Galbraith

Yuri stood at the desk: he felt strange wearing different clothes after all these years. The clothes belonged to a friend of his who had died. The boots chafed his feet but they were wearable.

He took the papers offered to him and went out through the doorway. The sun was trying to break through the fog. An eerie silence surrounded him. He walked over to the shuttle bus and climbed aboard. The bus shook its way to the arch between the high fences. He looked up and read the inscription on it. A tear rolled down his sunken cheek. The bus travelled forwards.

"We are the last. We are free," a man sitting in the row of seats over from him told him.

Yuri looked at him but said nothing. He turned his head and looked out of the window. Silver birch trees, so high they suddenly blocked out the light. Looking ahead he could see the small narrow road snaking away into the distance. He had a foreboding uncertainty about what lay ahead.

At Vladivostok he was told to leave the bus. He went to the train station and boarded the longest train he had ever seen. There were coaches with beds and another with a café. People were settling in for the journey. Yuri sat on a bed and claimed it as his.

Whistles were heard, a shout, and the train gradually left the station. He looked around at the many different people; they all seemed to be younger than him. He secured his meagre belongings, put his papers under his pillow, lay down and looked at the ceiling. Exhaustion caught up, and he fell asleep.

He awoke suddenly to an unfamiliar noise. It was another station; he stretched and rolled onto his side. He could see people walking through the carriage towards whatever they needed, looking for food or a visit to the toilet.

He got up, put his jacket on and his papers in his pocket, and went in search of sustenance.

As he accepted his tea and bread the man quoted a price. Yuri looked shocked. He produced a paper, handed it over, and the man examined it, looked at Yuri and dismissed him. Yuri went and sat at a table. The tables were filling up.

Two women sat opposite him. Something different about them, he was unsure what it was till one of them spoke to her friend, "That old man has had a hard life."

"Maybe he's a tramp," her friend answered. They both laughed quietly.

"I can understand some English," Yuri barked at them. They went quiet and looked ashamed. Yuri finished his tea and left the carriage. He went to freshen up and then sat on a seat in a small room, in a carriage that had no other occupants.

He looked out the window at the flatlands: fields and fields, a bare expanse of a huge land. Sometimes he saw the outlines of cottages and bigger houses. His eyes drank in the vastness, the peacefulness – and then the sheer terror of what he would do next seeped into his consciousness. He wearily walked back to his bed and lay down.

The days fell into a pattern of sorts. Many people left and boarded the train but Yuri remained. He had food when needed, but not much – being used to meagre portions over the years, he didn't need much. He kept to his solitude, wasn't used to people being friendly so when they knew he wouldn't speak they left him alone. He slept when needed and took a kind of comfort in the gentle rocking of the train. One day after a small meal he was sitting in the quiet compartment when a conductress came in and sat opposite him.

"I am Marina, the person who looks after the travellers and keeps them happy. I saw you before, and have to ask you a question."

Yuri looked at her with apprehension.

"I can tell a lot about people. I watch them often and can spot thieves, drug smugglers, and villains. I know you aren't one of them."

Yuri looked at her with a hint of a smile.

"An old soldier perhaps?" she asked with a small twinkle in her eye.

"National Service, many years ago," Yuri replied.

"But since then?" she asked. As she looked around she saw a tourist drop a piece of rubbish in the corridor opposite where they were sitting. She hurried out and shouted at the person. *She is ferocious*, Yuri thought.

She came back in and sat down again. "I run a good train, a tidy train, am respected by travellers and it should be so."

Yuri nodded, then said, "I have been in labour camps for a long time."

"I thought as much," Marina told him. "Since when and where?"

"KGB?" Yuri asked.

"No no, there is no KGB now." She told him.

"And you believe this?" Yuri asked looking astonished.

"There are many changes," she said.

"I can see that from the way the people behave now," he answered, "but I have been away for most of my life"

"I thought so," she remarked with a small nod.

"I was 24 years old when arrested. I was exiled in Magadan for many years. Hard to tell really, seasons come and go, you really are exiled there, the only way to and from it is by boat or plane. It was a very hard, harsh place. Then I was transferred to another camp near Vladivostock."

"What did you do to deserve such a sentence?"

Yuri shook his head and sunk his chin onto his chest.

"Wrong word at the wrong time I suspect," Marina said.

Yuri nodded.

"There were so many," Marina said, shaking her head gently. She paused and looked very thoughtful.

"The Berlin Wall has come down," she told him, "The east – well European east – is becoming westernised."

"No," Yuri shook his head, "This cannot be so."

"It is, you will see."

Yuri turned his head and looked out of the window, trying to absorb this news. Marina quietly left the coach.

The following day he was sitting in the same quiet place and he saw the outline of high wire fences and floodlights. He felt a tightening within himself: *it is another camp*. The train stopped at the station. "Perm," shouted a voice. Yuri half expected to be taken from the train and dragged away to it. He clutched his papers tightly but saw no one board the train. He was surprised, however, to see some people get off.

When the train continued its journey, Marina appeared and gave him a tray with borscht soup and bread. Yuri reached into his pocket.

"I don't accept coupons, and you will need them when you leave the train," she told him.

"Why did you bring me this?" Yuri asked.

"For surviving," she said simply. "I have work to do and can't chat all day." She walked away.

Yuri looked at the tray and smiled. After his meal he watched the landscape go by: many factories, industrial places and then another expanse of countryside.

The further east he travelled the more changes he saw: people were wearing different coloured coats and boots. He sensed a difference in the air just watching the people's movements and expressions. *Marina is right*, he thought.

He got off the train at Yaroslavl and saw new roads and many cars. He walked for a long time, passing orchards and gardens and small farmhouses until he reached a track, and he followed it until he saw his old house.

It was more or less a shell but still had a roof. The door was hanging on by one hinge. He went tentatively inside; the curtains were threads hanging on the broken window. There was a small pile of wood that used to be his furniture. Someone had been and used most of it for firewood. The place was dirty and very abandoned. His family was long gone.

He paused for a moment trying to gather his thoughts then walked into the small room at the back of the house, where he saw a shadow near the window. A tear slipped down his face as he recognised his old trombone case. He felt wonder that it could still be there. He opened the case and all the contents were as he left them. *Needs a clean,* he thought, closing the case.

He looked around one last time, unsure what to do now, but knowing he couldn't live here. As he left, he saw a piece of paper wedged in a small crack in the back of the front door, and prised it out. It was covered in clear cellophane of some sort. He unravelled it and seaw an address in Yaroslavl. *So nothing ventured*, he thought. He followed his instinct and walked for a long time to find the address. It was on the outskirts of what had now become a huge town. He was very weary.

On the way to the door he paused, and found strength from somewhere. He knocked on the door. A woman of about forty years old answered the door and looked inquisitively at him. Then she saw the trombone case and cried out. "Papa!" She almost screamed.

"You were just a baby when I last saw you," he told his daughter, Sasha.

"I don't remember you . . . but Mama told me many stories. We will have tea. You must tell me what happened." A young boy appeared beside her, "This is your grandson." she told Yuri.

Yuri went to shake the boy's hand, "What is your name?"

"Yuri."

Yuri felt choked and gave the boy a quick hug.

A few minutes later they were settled around the table.

"Mama died fifteen years ago"

Yuri nodded acknowledgement.

"My husband Sergei is working, you will meet him after his shift. Papa, Mama would not tell me why you were taken away." Sasha had tears flowing down her cheeks but went on, "I was told walls had ears in those days." She half laughed through her tears. She collected herself and went on, "I did not understand then. Now I do. But I still don't understand why you were taken away."

"I know Sasha, it all happened so fast."

"You were quite a famous songwriter and musician I was told," Sasha said.

"Yes I was. I was exiled because I would not write a song for Josef Stalin. I was sent to Magadan, a labour camp, where most people died."

Sasha clasped his hands in hers. "I have heard stories of that place," she admitted.

"After many seasons I was taken to a labour camp near Vladivostok, where I lost count of the years. Now I hear there have been many changes. I have seen some of them." He reached into his jacket pocket. "I have papers, so I can look for work."

"I think a rest is in order first," Sasha advised him.

"Can I see?" young Yuri asked, pointing to the trombone case.

"Yes of course," Yuri told him. He set the case on its side and opened it.

"It looks tarnished," young Yuri said.

"Oh I can fix that. I have the cream and the slide cream. A bit of patience and TLC and she'll play."

"Really?" Sasha asked looking surprised.

"Yes. I missed her too," Yuri commented, "Do you like music?" he asked the youngster.

"Yes, I can play the trombone at school but don't have my own one."

Sasha glared at her son.

"It is all right my dear. I will teach him how to restore and look after this trombone, and he will have one."

Sasha had a tear roll down her cheek, "I find it hard to believe you survived, Papa."

"There is an old Russian saying: *Wherever God has planted us, we must learn how to flower.*" Yuri took her hand in his and added, "I am no longer a number, I am Yuri Soloviev, and I am very happy to be here."

From the Lighthouse

Kenny Gilchrist

You sailed away in the forties,
to live a bountiful life in Canada.

Though you sailed over to the
after life this year.
Obols were placed for Charon.

The lighthouse remains,
the constant,
shining its beam at night.

Connecting family members,
still sailing in life's stormy seas.

The Dance of our Lives

Ruth Gilchrist

A long time ago you took me dancing,
you with a gleam in your eye.

Remember how we danced at our wedding?
You had such pride in your eye.

We danced with our friends for house warming,
you with the whole world in your eye.

With our young family we had no time for dancing,
you went to work with bleary eye.

But time passed and you took me dancing,
you with a sparkle in your eye.

The grandchildren lead us a 'merry dance'.
And you? You had mischief in your eye!

Now we sit, watch the young ones dancing,
you have a faraway look in your eye.

I will soon be dancing on my own,
but you: you'll have peace in your eye.

Mackenzie Point

Billy Graham

It had been a relief to both of us when I saw my grandfather off on the train back to his beloved Highlands. He had not been impressed with our cities with their rubbish strewn streets: folk with an inherent fear of litter bins, passing without a word or a smile – others in cars following one another like lemmings.

"You know where I bide, Ian," he said, leaning out of the carriage window. And I knew by the way he had said it that he would not be back. I also knew the effort it had taken the old man to journey here to attend my mother and young brother's funeral, the result of a road accident.

So here I was again after ten years: at the promontory known locally as MacKenzie Point, where my grandfather lived.

Oh, how my brother Harry and I had looked forward to those school summer holidays. Pirates sailing in grandfather's skiff, in waters so clear that I was convinced I could walk on the bottom, or watching seals by the rocks around the bay. Journeying to the seam of white quartzite on one of the steep hills, which one day to us would be a frozen waterfall in the Arctic, or on another, the hidden treasure of King Solomon's mines. All this we had enjoyed until I turned fifteen, when it all suddenly appeared to be quite boring, and all I wanted to do was stay at home with my pals.

I fed the steering wheel through my hands as I turned the corner, and there it was, the white washed cottage, just as I had last seen it as a boy.

The door was open and from where I had stopped the car I could see my grandfather sitting reading at the table by the lantern light on this fine summer night, with the sun sinking blood red into the sea.

"I have been expecting you, Ian," he said without looking up. "You will find some soup on the stove, not as good as your granny used to make, but passable."

I put down my overnight bag, wondering as I greeted my grandfather, how he knew of my coming, as I had only just decided that Friday morning to visit him, but I knew better than to ask.

"It's been a long time, grandfather," I said as I supped.

The old man with the mop of silver hair sat puffing contentedly on his pipe. "Aye, but I knew you would come back some day."

I felt myself blush as I said, "Now I know I never should have stopped. Harry loved coming here. We had some good times together. It was me who usually spoiled things, like . . ."

He stopped me. "Like the day Harry was accused of stealing yon apple from auld Stewart the grocer?" The old man shook his head sadly. "A bad day yon, Ian. Even after the wee laddie had explained that he thought you had paid for it with the rest of the groceries, you did not speak up for him. You knew he had not stolen it, and there was auld Stewart telling folk he had caught him red handed and that possession was nine tenths of the law, and so on and so on. And it was only because that he came from a respectable family that he did not call in the law."

Despite the time that had elapsed since that awful day, I still felt ashamed. Grandfather was right, I knew my brother had not stolen the damned apple, but just for once I had wanted to see my grandparents' faces when they found out that their darling little cherub was not so perfect after all. It had hurt them, but not as much as it had hurt wee Harry at what I had done.

Anxious to change the subject I rushed to ask. "How are you coping on your own now that granny . . . ?"

The old man knocked dottle from his pipe and pointed at the miniature carriage clock standing on the mantle shelf. "I have never wound it up since her passing."

I gave a little shudder. The time on its face said eleven twenty nine, the exact minute of her passing. I asked no more.

Later, when my grandfather had said his goodnight, I stood looking out of the window in the tiny bedroom Harry and I had shared as boys, at the moon rising from the loch, casting ghostly shadows on the sleeping hills, and I though again of the good times we all had had. There was only my grandfather and I left now. I drew in a deep breath, and even in the tiny room so filled with memories, I smelled the air so unique to this part of the Highlands.

The next day my grandfather and I did everything Harry and I had done as boys – fishing from the skiff, sailing up the bay, feeling again the magic of Mackenzie Point, tinged with the sadness that those halcyon days were no more, and that granny, my mother and brother were not here to share those precious holidays once more, nor would they ever do so again.

Understanding my mood, my grandfather said, as he turned the little boat out to sea,

"I know you miss them Ian, but life must go on. We are only here for a wee while, even that the good Lord has seen fit to give me a wee bit longer than most, my life is but as a mayfly to all of this." He said it in his soft Highland lilt, sweeping a hand at the majestic mountains and the vast expanse of the sea.

I knew I should have made my way back to the city the next day, but this I could not do, as it was Sunday, the Sabbath, so in order not to offend my grandfather I told him that I would be leaving early Monday morning, apologising and promising to stay longer next time. His only reaction was to give me a knowing smile.

The next morning I closed the bedroom door behind me, locking in those memories until I came again. In the kitchen, my eyes roamed around the sparsely furnished room as if seeing things there for the very first time, aware of the absence of all those 'must have' things I had believed to be essential to a modern way of life, and suddenly I envied the old man his contentment.

Although I had risen early, my grandfather was nowhere to be seen. I finished breakfast and walked up the brae to where I knew he had sat on the same rock every morning, at peace with the world, puffing on his pipe, eyes fixed on the wee burn below, and it was there I found him again.

"So, you will be away then?" he said, his eyes still on the tumbling burn.

"Yes, but I will be back, Grandfather. It has been great to be here again. I'll make it longer next time."

He half turned to look at me. "Aye, you do that Ian. But will you do something for me?"

"Of course," I said, clearing my throat.

"Take the wee clock with you."

My eyes opened wide in astonishment. "I can't do that Grandfather, the clock was yours and granny's."

"Time does not stand still like yon wee clock, Ian. Take it, and be reminded that you must make the best of your life, for you will not always be young, and time passes so quickly, more so as you grow older," he added with a sigh.

"Thanks Grandfather, I will treasure it. It will always remind me of you and MacKenzie Point." The old man nodded his head and turned away.

On my way to my car, clutching the precious clock in one hand and my holdall in the other, I saw two men walking up the path towards me: one, a small middle age rotund man, the other in the uniform of a policeman.

"May I ask who you are sir?" the policeman asked firmly, but politely.

"Ian MacKenzie. My grandfather bides in the cottage back there." I pointed with the clock, in direction of the house.

Both men's eyes drifted to the miniature, and I held it up to proudly show them. "He gave me this as a parting gift. I am on my way back home, to Edinburgh."

The officer of the law half turned to his companion, though it still was to me that he spoke. "And when would this be, Mister MacKenzie, that old Ewen gave you that?" he asked pointing at the clock.

"A few minutes ago," I replied, puzzled by the question.

"And your grandfather, where would he be now, laddie?" the other man asked, looking over my shoulder.

"Where he usually is at this time of day, up the brae by the burn."

"Then we will have a word with the man." The policeman stepped passed me as he spoke.

I turned, and without speaking, we made our way to where I had last seen my grandfather sitting on the rock, though this time the place was deserted.

"He must have gone for a stroll round the brae – he does this you know," I hurried to assure them, catching the note of anxiety in my voice.

"That as it may be, but you still insist that old MacKenzie gave you that clock this very minute?" This time the policeman voice held no warmth.

"That I do, and when he returns he will verify it," I flashed at him, now angry that he was accusing me of having stolen my own grandfather's clock. "And why should he not do so?" I spluttered.

The officer's brown eyes stared coldly at me.

"Because, old Ewen Mackenzie passed away three days ago, and now lies down yonder in the village, God rest his soul, that is why."

I stared at the man in sheer disbelief, unaware of clutching the clock so tightly in my hand, as the other man said firmly, "Caught red handed Constable, would you not say?"

And as he spoke, the clock chimed the half hour, and once again I thought of my brother Harry.

Welcome

Jamie Graham

I can't go home though you'd like me to.
What did I ever do to you?
My clothes are old, but my heart is not.
I just want a piece of what you've got:

To go to school and learn new things,
to play in the park on the slide and swings,
you punch me though and it hurts so bad,
I wish that I could tell my Dad.

But he got killed and so did my sister –
she was stone cold dead when I last kissed her.
I should be safe at last away from fear,
but when I go to play you're always near.

You're older, taller and I hate you
for making my new life a misery too.
What did I ever do to you?
But you ripped my jacket and stole my shoes.

I can't even go to the shop on my own.
When Mum's out at work I cry all alone.
My Dad would beat you if he was here,
and make *you* cry these thousand tears.

But instead I feel worthless and afraid,
just like I did before I came to this place.
I've been through hell but I don't feel strong –
this little bird has lost his song.

I can't go home though you'd like me to.
What did I ever do to you?
My clothes are old, but my heart is not.
I just want a piece of what you've got.

Heralds of Spring

Cathie Gray

Winter sent out her
Heralds of Spring,
the lovely sweet snowdrops,
their tiny white flowers
spiking through the ground
braving the cold, the wind,
the rain and the snow.

The Heralds of Spring
peeking out from corners,
sheltering under trees,
emphasising their sweet shyness.

The Heralds of Spring,
a sight most welcome
on a cold damp winter morn,
give hope of another year.
A beginning, with their brightness
and sweet shyness.

Wilderness Tales

Penny Hext

Every kid has a Teddy Bear – except that mine was a koala – called Tazzie. His fur had worn down to tufts from being clamped under my arm. Tazzie Bear was my best friend. Together we grew up beneath the wide blue skies of Tasmania.

Home was a corrugated tin hut on the edge of green forest wilderness. It was a long, long way from anywhere. Even the mainland. You trapped your own meat, baked your own bread, and chopped your own firewood. The road was dirt-track. At sundown, those tracks crawled with kangaroos and wallabies and wombats and quolls and other bush-animals I couldn't even name. Kookaburras mobbed the eucalyptus trees like punks.

There were snakes too. You had to learn to deal with them quick. If you didn't, you were dead. Simple as. We lived too far out in the bush to be able to medicate snakebite. So a bad snakebite could be lethal, if you were unlucky. But you had to be pretty unlucky. The snakes weren't stupid. I hardly ever saw a whole one. Just a tail sliding into a crevice.

I never set foot out of doors without a hat clapped to my head and the stern admonition to mind where I was going. From so high, it was drummed into me: people disappear into that wilderness.

They still do.

Where we lived was right on the frontier of ancient Gondwanaland: the Tarkine rainforest. Vast tracts are still uncharted. It was full of trees and ferns and rivers and waterfalls – a primeval Eden – home to all sorts of wildlife. Tasmanian tigers even, so they said. Though they were supposed to be extinct.

We were settlers, father said. We couldn't afford to be picky Poms.

* * *

My mother was an arachnophobe. I didn't know the name for it then. But that's what she was. I remember her face when she caught sight of a spider. How her eyes rounded like golfballs. How her face stretched and elongated. She had a horror of spiders, a fear which she tried to push down and control. She'd never scream out loud. But a moan would sometimes leak from the side of her mouth.

They weren't that big really, the spiders, but some could jump. Some could bite. Some could even spit long distance. And every of them moved straight for her.

There were lots of spiders in our place. They crawled up through the gaps in the floorboards, and dropped down from our rackety tin roof. They hid behind the picture frames, underneath the toilet seat in the dunny, and inside the broom cupboard. There was no safe place. As fast as you brushed and swept, they'd be spinning their webs and weaving their funnels once more. Reclaiming their territory.

I would toddle – and later run – fast as I could to where my mother cowered and hold onto her knees for dear life. It helped calm her, she said. Sometimes, it would take an hour or more to coax her down from the chair or the table that she had climbed onto, as the spider scooted around the living room looking for an escape. Or legged it up the walls. You could hear it tick-a-tacking as it went.

By the age of five I'd got good at catching them. I had to. By evening, our shack would have one, two, or more jars, each imprisoning an enraged arachnid. Red eyes popping with fury. Occasionally a bigger one would rootle its leg out, one leg at a time, from its glass prison and pitch an escape. It was the ones that stood their ground: up on hind legs, jaws working, that scared me most. They could spit with hair-splitting precision. Those I let go.

My father's most pressing task, upon his return from a day's work in the bush, would be to get rid of the spiders. There and then. My mother wouldn't take 'no'. She refused to make supper until the place had been de-spidered.

Not that it seemed to make any difference to the next day.

As I grew older, wiser, I wondered . . . did he actually Do the Deed? Or just shuggle those jars back out into the yard?

It would be quicker. Plus he was a softy.

When the shack fell silent after dark, you would sometimes hear a muffled, hesitant shuffle across the corrugated tin ceiling. Or worse, a whumpf down onto the bare boards, as you lay abed. Trying not to listen as one scouted.

The worst was when it went still.

Because it didn't mean that nothing was out there.

It meant one lay await – plotting – for the right moment.

Since neither parent could be trusted in a spider emergency, I slept with a jam jar and a stick by my bed. Just in case . . . I had a particular horror of falling asleep with my mouth wide open and a spider somehow finding its way into me. Whilst I lay oblivious . . .

When I ask my mother what it was that brought her back – finally – from Tasmania, it wasn't the red dust. Or the eucalyptus trees. Or even the snakes.

It was the spiders.

* * *

Dartmoor. The Ten Pound Poms' return. That's us: my mother, my father and me. It's Xmas. It's freezing. We're camping in my grandmother's prized parlour, back home in Pom-land. All of us squashed in together.

Happy Days.

The Big Tip was where my grandparents lived in a two up, two down, with an outside privy. Two rows of quarrymen's houses, all exactly alike. The house was on the slagheap, like all the other houses. It was granite they quarried there. Of course it wasn't really called the Big Tip – but that's the name it went by locally, and it stuck.

It was home to a whole community who lived just outside Princetown, in the heart of the moor, with just an old stone track leading to it over bog. When he was a lad, my father used to while away a day by counting the cars that drove past in the distance. It was never more than the fingers of one hand.

Home. It both was – and was not – so very different from the one I'd just left.

Fog for flies. Bog for wilderness. Crows for kookaburras . . .

The spiders follow us all the way from Down Under. My mother cowers – she's not managed to find a chair in time – as a spider spritzes across the stone-flagged floor of the kitchen directly towards her.

He's got her in his sights.

I pounce and capture it in my bare hands, whilst her fingers flutter to her lips. Her face drains of colour. She'll need a lie down after this. My grandmother tsks. She has no time for such nonsense.

I edge into the yard to let it run away. I like penny spiders: they're so tiny.

It's a grim yard beneath a steel sky. The air bites like a tigersnake's smile. I glance up, spider forgotten, as white stuff drifts down soft about my shoulders. It dissolves into a silver puddle at my feet.

Snow. I have never seen it before. But I've heard about it. My mother read me *The Snow Queen* at home at night on the edge of Gondwanaland . . . So this is it. I stand entranced. Face upturned, I allow myself to be coated in snowflakes. I stick my tongue out. My bare fingers tingle. My nose tickles.

Soon our tiny yard is covered in an inch of snow all over.

Still it falls.

Beyond our walls and the Big Tip, the bog has disappeared beneath a crust of snow. The white has transformed into grey eddies. It blizzards a short while. Squidge metamorphoses into crunch.

The yard door swings open: my father returns covered in snow, grinning like a schoolboy. In an instant he sheds his grey clerical self along with his suit. He whisks me off sledging: turn and turn about, with all the other kids and their dads.

Everybody's muffled in hats and gloves and scarves, shrieking. We start a snowball fight: Big Tippers versus Quarrymen. The air thrums with the soft thud of snowballs. There's an 'on holiday' feeling. The smaller kids build snowmen – which the older ones kick over. Grandpa sucks on his pipe with his elbows on the yard wall and grunts.

We win. And pelt the Quarrymen back up their own track. Home.

My dad stops to help one of the smaller kids with his snowman. It stops the older ones stomping it down.

It's snowing harder now. Getting whiter again, in a swirly sort of way.

Slowly, softly, the snow is transforming treacherous liquid bog into solid walkable terrain.

Because I am with my father, I am granted immunity: carte blanche to do what I want. We could journey into the unknown across the wilderness . . .

A Christmas present worth having.

At last.

Kimberley Kim

Frances Hider

The last time we saw Kimberley Kim was in the summer of 2009. Calvin spotted her and called me down to the sitting room. She was curled nose to tail on the old green chair in front of the patio windows. Her brown and white coat, fluffed and scruffy as it had always been, made her look more like a rug dog than a springer spaniel. For a second or two my heart flipped. She was back. As we watched, she slid off the chair, slipped behind the sofa and was gone.

That she sloped away wasn't really a surprise. Kimberley Kim had died ten years earlier. We buried her in the shelterbelt, her unmarked grave now lost in the ever-changing landscape of vegetation and trees.

In life, she wasn't a big dog. She was born with an undershot jaw, which didn't hinder her ability to eat and 'eating' was her obsession. One Christmas, when she was still a young dog, we found her in her bed curled round a box of twelve deluxe mince pies. Unable to prize open the packaging she slept protecting them as she might have done a litter of twelve spaniel puppies.

When she was an eight-week-old Calvin went to collect her from her breeder, a local gamekeeper. She was the last to leave from a basket once full of romping springer pups. Her undershot jaw made her unfit for breeding, and although we don't know for sure, we suspect she may very well have been destroyed had Calvin not taken her in as a pet.

In her time, Kimberley Kim was the dog who found Action Man. This sturdy commando was lost in the hay field the day before by a small boy who couldn't sleep without him. Kimberley Kim could be relied on to be back at your side on the first whistle. She liked to play fetch with a ball although eventually she was overtaken by a younger dog and lost interest. She was a gentle dog who was only ever heard to growl once when a new puppy sharing her bed edged in too vigorously.

Kimberley's one less endearing feature was a penchant for horse dung, which she scoffed down in quantity on a near daily basis. As she aged and became somewhat jowly, the debris of her pungent feasts caught in the sides of her mouth to linger fetid on her breath. She was 17 years old when she died. It was a shock to us, as it had seemed as if she would live forever.

To say I saw her that summer morning ten years after her death stretches the imagination. She was barely there. Her presence was more of a warm feeling, the collision of a memory and a wish. The sceptic in me knows the likely explanation for her sighting was a trick of the early morning sunlight. Being quick from sleep, and short on canine companionship, I let the natural order of the day give way to the supernatural. It was something of a *folie à deux* as both Calvin and I conjured up her image.

Treasured in her life, Kimberley Kim was so very missed in death. It was as if she gifted us one last encounter that day. When she slipped away behind the sofa it wasn't the pungent odour of horse dung that hung in the air but the bittersweet scent of nostalgia that lingered to haunt me.

James Whistled to Himself . . .

James Inglis

James whistled to himself as he wandered through the Forest gathering up herbs – especially his favourite, sodjers wort – and was now some distance from the camp. That didn't worry him though: he now knew the Forest as well as anyone in the camp, perhaps better, as his wanderings were off the deer paths and trails in the search for his herbs. Suddenly he stopped. He saw movement, up ahead at a clearing, by a small stream. A man was spear fishing in the stream and a dog was splashing about in the water beside him. James was about to backtrack away before he was seen, or smelt by the dog, but froze as just then the dog came out of the water and vigorously shook itself to clear the water from its fur. Its fur was long and as it shook itself the fur rotated around its body, back and forth, with water spray flying off in all directions.

"Cut that oot, Bracken," the man cried, as water spray went all over him, drenching him. "And you're not helping, scaring aw the fish away with your splashing aboot, what'll we eat if I dinnae catch any fish, you want anither hungry night?" The dog had stopped shaking itself and stood still and sniffed the air, several times, then barking, rushed towards where James was standing behind some bushes, beside a pine tree. It came right up to the tree and continued to bark, its long, broad snout pointing directly at James, but it didn't attack him. The man came running up, fishing spear in his hands and pointing at James. "Come oot from there," he ordered, "or I'll gie the dog the order to attack, and he's a fierce beast, he'll rip yi to shreds."

James cautiously came out from behind the tree, watching the dog with his every step. "Call yer hound off, I mean yi nae hairm, see I've nae weapon," said James, raising his arms high and wide to show he was unarmed.

"Quiet, Bracken, quiet noo. Whit is you doing here?" asked the young lad, for that's what he was, James now saw, not a grown man at all.

"I'm gaithering herbs, see in this basket," and James held out his basket of herbs for the lad to see. "I might ask you the same, lad, you're a bit young to be traipsing around these woods all by yourself, whit are ye doing here?"

"I'll ask the questions, I've got a spear and a vicious dog!"

"So you have, so you have, but I've got something to eat, have you?"

The boy hesitated. "What you got?" he asked anxiously, suddenly no longer aggressive.

"Pit your spear down and invite me to sit down with you, nice and freendly like, and I'll show you."

The lad thought about it, giving James a good look over, went back to his small fire by the stream. "Let's see whit you have to eat then!"

James followed him over, set himself down beside the fire, and rummaging under all the herbs, brought out a leaf parcel from the bottom of the basket. He opened the large leaf and inside was a hunk of bread, a large piece of cheese, a big raw onion and an apple.

"Wow!" The boy exclaimed, his tongue licking over his lips at the sight, as if he had just been shown a banquet.

"Help yersell," said James, breaking off a chunk of bread and a piece of cheese and stuffing both into his mouth. The boy needed no further encouragement and quickly tore off a large bit of bread and cheese and softly moaned as he chewed, while breaking pieces off to give to his dog, which devoured the morsels without chewing! James cut the onion and the apple into halves with a small knife he brought from the basket and gestured to the boy to again help himself. The boy bit into the apple and juice ran down his chin, which was quickly mopped up by a flicking tongue and the apple disappeared within seconds. The onion was next; it got the same treatment, with just a hint of the boy's face screwing up at the sour tang of the onion, especially coming straight after the sweetness of the apple. There was some bread and cheese still left on the leaf and the boy looked at James, who smiled and nodded, and two snake-like hands reached down, gathered up the remains, and dropping some to Bracken, the boy quickly devoured the rest. "That were gid!" he exclaimed, "In fact, mare than gid, blidy great!" The boy belched and grinned and went over to the stream, followed by the dog, and both drank some cool fresh water to wash down the feast.

"Time for introductions I think. Ma name's James, I'm a smithy just like ma faither and I com frae round here."

"I'm caud Edgar, I never kent my faither, nor my mither, always been on my own. I worked at a farm in Northum'erland, working, working, awe the time. I hated it, 'cept when I got to work wi the horses and that were gid but then I ran."

"You dinnae sound like any Englishman I've ever met, you sound near the same as me. What did you run awa fer?" asked James.

"I was a slave," he replied, seemingly rather surprised at the question, "you get beaten a' the time, get fed same as pigs, yi work till you die, or you run! I ran."

"How did you end up here?"

"'Fore I ran, I kent that I would get caught if I did run, cause where could I run to? But then, I heard talk about the Scotch folk fighting for their freedom and I could nae stop thinking aboot that. Night after night, thinking aboot fighting for yer freedom, I dreamed every night aboot it, cause they canna stop you thinking and dreamin, can they? So the first chance I got, I ran. I headed north, as all I knew was Scotland was in the north, and here I am. Is this Scotland?"

"Yea it is, just the Borders area mind, we're only aboot ten miles from England. Why did ye bring the dug wi ye?"

"I never brote him, I found him! I skirted a big toon some time ago and I cam across him lying doon in a ditch. I nearly passed him by, being the colours he is and very dirty too."

James looked across at the dog and noted its camouflaged colouring of black with shades of brown, irregular stripes and small patches of white and a gingery colour.

"I thooght he was deid at first, but he gave a whimper when he see'd me, so I knew he wisnae. I pulled him oot the ditch and half carried and half dragget him to a nearby stream where I pit him in the water and cleaned him. He had a guid drink o water there as I checked to see if he was injured, but I could'na find anything! I had a few scraps o' chicken I pinched frae the last fairm I passed the day b'fore, geed him some, well maist really, and we've been ti gither since. I geed him his name, as he's the same colour as yon bracken turns at the end o' summer. We're freends!" Edgar leaned over and hugged the dog.

"That's some story, Edgar, you've had a bit o' an adventure, but what'll yi dae now?"

"I'll keep goin till I meet folk who are fightin fir their freedom, and join them, I suppose!"

James looked at the lad, a wee innocent, wi a dream! He smiled and a thought came to him, *I suppose I could tak him back wi me, feed him up a bit at least? Why no?*

"Edgar, how wid yi like ti come back wi me? I'll gie yi a meal ti fill yer belly fu ti burstin, aye, and Bracken tae."

"Really? Fit ti burstin?"

"Aye, come on, but yi baith have ti be a bit quiet though, okay? We can talk as we go, but nae shoutin or that." All three set off, James leading and Edgar behind, talking to him, to the dog, to the trees, to everything.

Boats in the Harbour

Gordon Jamieson

This is the tale that was told to me,
by a man with a toothless grin
as he sat along the harbour wall,
repaired a torn net, again and again.

He pulled an auld clay cutty frae his pouch,
filled it up wi backy, black,
struck a match, gave a cough and a spit,
and then began to tell:

"I remember when the harbour was stappet foo
wi boats of a sizes, some shiny, some new,
wi wonderful names like *Bonny Lass* an *Thorntree* –
sae sweet o line fur the eye to see.

On a guid day when the sun is high,
you can smell the sea
that smells o weed, an oil, an fish,
soon shrouded in the smoke an reek o coming day.

I remember when the harbour was foo
o Fifies an Yoles a-drying their sails,
wi some pulled ower
tae gee thir bottoms a paint.

A sad reflection of earlier days
wi maist o the fleet all faded away,
noo replaced wi the throb o Diesel oil –
the prawn boats are a that's left here now.

I remember when ringers filled the harbour foo,
sae trig an neat at beam an bow –
their paintwork flashing wi the sea
as they wait for the tide tae set them free.

I remember when the month o September wad come,
an the fishermen wad parade through the toon,
an the folk wad walk, an dance, an sing,
fur it was time for the Box meeting tae be here again.

The grey-green sea still slaps the pier heid,
the sea walls dashed wi white spray,
fish boxes stacked along the way,
there waiting fur the catch, fur you and me."

Makar

Mary Johnston

Fair scunnert the muse widna come,
I took a waalk an cam upon a buss
hingin wi ripe berries tycin me ti taste them:
tho stobs scarted ma nyakit airms,
I raxed up, poo'ed a puckle,
stappit foo ma moo, shut ma een
an mindit on langsyne simmer days:
twis then I hid the notion ti mak jam.

A whilie sin I'd deen aat:
mibbe I'd tint the knack,
feart it widna jeel,
poo'ed the wrang berries,
(bonny tho they wir)
hid I ower deen the sugar,
nae eneuch heat naith the pan,
wis ma steerin ower roch,
mibbe needit a cannier han?

Wytin, tho hard ti thole,
pyed aff in the eyn;
aa the redd-up frae the berries
ye coodna see afore,
in a fite, reamie scum
cam floatin ti the tap:
I scraped it aff an threw't awa -
a rollin bile o rubies rumblt roon the pan!

I spooned a suppie intil a sasser,
wi ma pinkie scooped it up,
taste an smell tore inti ma senses-
I hidna tint the knack!
I set the jam aside ti set,
fair teen on the muse wis back.

Glossary

stobs-*thorns*
scarted-*scratched*
nyakit-*bare;*
puckle-*some/few*
mindit-*remembered*
tint the knack
-lost the art
eneuch-*enough*
redd-up-*tidying up;*
fite-*white*
reamie-*foamy*
bile-*boil*
suppie-*small portion*
sasser-*saucer*
fair-*absolutely*
teen on-*delighted*

"Hallo, Doll"

Anne Jones

I watch his lips take the shape of a kiss round the word 'doll' and smile, run my hands the length of the lurex sleeve of a dress. He salivates, I've done it, and I'm in, with no charge because I arrive early. I search for the Ladies and behold my image in many mirrors. The regime had taken hours; my wig is lop sided, so is my bra, a false eyelash has sprung loose, my toes in the points of red shoes are yelling, "set me free." My sodden armpits mottle the self tan. All these obstacles and still I am amazing. The multiples reflected are beyond exciting. I set to, repairing the damage a short walk has done. I pout many pouts, refresh the lip gloss, flick my blonde fringe, pull the loose black spider from my eyelid then glue it back on again. I'm now surrounded by busy prettying dolls. I'm in heaven, falling in love with them all -all -all.

The Artist Formerly Known as Hitler

Jeff Kemp

When I travelled
back in time,
I did the usual things
– shot Hitler,
stopped the plague –
then returned to clocks
still chiming the hour
of my departure.

Sated from my
future sampling
of the past
– its decisive flavour
laced with pre-destiny –
I saw at a glance
that nothing
was askance.

Quick fire actions
can't decontaminate
backwards
– with a Hitler water-colour on the wall
and pet rats running over the floor –
I was reassured
by continuity's
absolute over-rule.

History's imprisoned in itself
like the chicken
and the egg
– Adolph H is a famous artist,
rodents are cute enough to die for –
scratching time's surface
surely can't destabilize
its core.

Cold Feet!

Graham Leake

I *could* have been a mountaineer,
scaling heights both far and near.
Seeking out a risky climb,
and facing death time after time.
But, honesty forbids conceit;
I know that I would get cold feet.

I *could* have been a toreador:
attacking bulls – creating gore.
But, though I might believe I could,
I really know I never would,
for honesty forbids conceit;
I know that I would get cold feet.

Hang gliding is a thrilling sport,
if thermals help you as they ought.
Swooping skywards, free as a bird . . .
but – no; that really is absurd.
Honesty forbids conceit;
I know that I would get cold feet.

I *could* have been a tight-rope walker
(less arduous than a deer-stalker)
high in the air, no need to fret.
Who cares about a safety net?
Honesty, though, forbids conceit;
I know that I would get cold feet.

I *could* have been so many things
once free of Mother's apron strings.
Channel swimmer, caving buff,
lion tamer, rugby tough . . .
But, honesty forbids conceit;
I know that I would get cold feet.

Now that I am old and grey,
I must accept I've had my day.
There's not much risk I'm fit to take;
they'll soon be merry at my wake.
They'll put me in a grave so neat
and then I'll surely have cold feet!

Then

Elsie Lindsay

War clouded our childhood
cast shadows over our games
darkening the light.
The bogeyman
lurked in the blackout,
the wail of the siren
tainted our dreams.
A drab Lenten-time,
we sat round meagre tables
listening to myths of abundance,
imagining bananas,
cream cakes and chocolate.
We did without.
After the war,
the sun shone
for a while,
the bells rang, bonfires blazed.
Our long-absent fathers,
coming home to bunting and banners,
seemed smaller and more distant
than before.

The Time Thing

Lyn Livingstone

The weight of time can apply to boredom –
or a prison term.
Or be the heaviness of, and the waiting
for ill health to pass – or life to end.
Time may drag to a standstill waiting
for a declaration of love or exam results.
It's an immovable tyrant if there's no news
loved ones survived disaster.
Time's the abyss between heights of pain at a birth.

Thing is, time will shrink or expand
according to events.
Better to flicker and burn than fizzle and fade
The right attitude only goes so far.
Bad ageing imposes the heaviest time,
this, a burden carried from one day to the next:
waiting for help to eat, to bathe – for someone to call;
hear a voice in the corridor, or through a wall.
Then the slow disappearing behind closed shades.

On the Scale and on the Bus

Bruce Lumsden

Paul was definitely 'on the scale' as they say. His attention to detail could be unnerving, and his passion for accuracy made conversations with him difficult at times. That apart, he was able to carry on as normal. I know I can be difficult," he would say, "but I can't help it."

Paul was well-suited to his job as a teacher of History. It was a subject that consumed him and his enthusiasm rubbed off on his pupils, despite their sniggering behind his back. He would animate his lessons with mimicked accents and actions, bringing otherwise dull subjects to life.

His life was run by two rules: routine, and the filling of every waking hour with fruitful mental or physical activity. Whether it be running or swimming to tire his body, or chess and politics to tire his brain, Paul would crack under the stress of life if a strict regime were not in place.

Up in the morning slightly late as usual, he had a hurried breakfast of tea and toast on the run, so to speak. A frantic car journey to school, then work. On the frequent days when the car wouldn't start, the bus to school was an alternative that routinely suited Paul. Routine was the order of the day – not living in a rut. He could walk to the bus stop in 3 minutes and pile on to the overcrowded 7.45. Usually he would have to stand for the 23 minute journey. At the bus stop he would meet, or rather see, the same folk every time. He could work out in his mind roughly how long they had been there by their place in the queue, in relation to the bald headed man in his 30s or so, who was always whistling. Paul had established that his fellow traveller would whistle the last song he heard on Radio 2 before leaving his house, so Paul could work out when he left his house to walk to the stop, assuming an average time folk might take to walk. This was not entirely accurate, which irritated him, but nevertheless it would occupy his brain enough till the bus arrived.

Today, the car did not start again and it was raining... a double blow. As he walked in the rain to the bus stop his brain tussled with another conundrum – would he be dryer if he ran to the bus shelter and so spent less time in the rain, but hit each rain drop harder, causing it to soak in more? Or if he walked and took longer in the rain, but allowed some of the raindrops to bounce off? This had puzzled Paul for quite some time but he concluded that he would need a control traveller to accurately compare results on a single day – then a measure of absorption, possibly weighing clothes at the start and conclusion of the journey – and so on. Leaving this unsolved, he arrived at the bus shelter, to stand behind the whistler.

The whistler was last in the queue and Paul boarded the bus after him, paid his fare and sat in the remaining seat next to him. They had never spoken before and Paul saw no reason to change that.

He was never at ease in the company of his fellow travellers. There was an element of being slightly out of control with whatever was going on. The woman in front of him had long shoulder length hair that she was perpetually arranging from perfect – to perfect – then back to perfect again. He wanted to let her know that her hair was perfect, but that sort of thing had led to problems before, so he changed his gaze to the youngster opposite him. He was plugged into his music and the nodding of his head led Paul to conjecture what he was listening to. He thought he could recognise the beat, but it could be one of a hundred tunes. Should he tap him on the shoulder and ask, or would that be weird? That would seem weird to others – not him, but nevertheless he let it go.

Then it started.

The whistler was quietly half-whistling, half-blowing his morning tune. Paul's ears tuned in and his brain locked on to the obvious questions. What was it, and what had he heard after it before leaving the house? He knew the song, but its name escaped him this morning. He thought hard but could not bring the name to mind. He ran through the tune in his head, including, he thought, the middle 8 – but still nothing. Usually a word would jump out to him and trigger the memory.

The whistler was still blowing away, restricting his whistling to the melody, over and over again.

Passengers left and joined the bus at each stop, but Paul was unable to divert his mind from that tune. He knew it well and liked it, but could not get a handle on the name. He thought about asking the whistler, but that would be cheating, would it not? No, he had to remember. Going through the alphabet and imagining the song title at every letter often worked… but not this morning.

The whistler stopped. Paul could not believe it. He needed the repetition of that damned tune so he could remember. He began to fidget in his seat, becoming slightly agitated, and the whistler turned and spoke.

"You alright?" the whistler enquired

This was Paul's chance to ask the question.

"Yes, I'm just thinking of something that's irritating me."

The whistler rose out his seat and stood ready to get off at the next stop. Paul had another two stops to go, but his legs stood him up, and as soon as they did, the song title entered his brain.

"*Sweet home Alabama*!" His mouth spurted out the title towards the whistler.

"Eh?"

"The song you were whistling. *Sweet home Alabama.* You must have heard it on the radio this morning."

"No . . . I wasn't whistling that."

"Yes you were." Paul was becoming indignant, and a nuisance.

"What's it to you anyway?"

"I – I – I –," Paul stuttered. ". . . I was just trying to remember the name."

"I was whistling that song about werewolves in London." And with that, the bus stopped and the whistler left . . . with Paul dumbstruck.

"It *was Sweet home Alabama*," Paul said, to the bemusement of the surrounding passengers. Obviously embarrassed by speaking his thoughts, Paul left the bus one stop early and walked the extra distance to school.

None of the staff shared Paul's taste in music or radio stations, so it had to wait till he got home before he could confirm what he knew.

He looked on computer at the playlist for the morning show, and there it was in black and white: *Sweet home Alabama.* He was right . . . yes . . . the whistler was wrong. Paul would tell him at the next opportunity. Paul's eyes did not see *Werewolves of London* on the previous page.

The chance to speak to the whistler did not come soon.

Paul travelled by bus for the next eight days but there was no sign of the whistler – till, on the ninth day, he was there waiting at the stop, half way up the queue. It was raining hard and Paul had experimented with running to the bus stop and examining his clothing for wetness, but the sight of the whistler brought it all home.

"*Sweet home Alabama.*" He spoke loudly to the bus queue. "I looked it up on the web."

"*Werewolves of London*, so did I," replied the whistler, and entered the bus.

"You're wrong," replied Paul, as the driver let him know that there was no more room and he would have to wait for the next bus.

"No, you're wrong," the whistler mouthed as he smiled through the bus window, and the bus pulled away from the stop.

Paul was not upset at missing the bus; he could cope with the wait for the next one. He had won the argument and was glowing with self-pride.

The whistler was delighted at the opportunity to settle matters with the fruitcake at the bus stop who tried to tell him what he was whistling. It was still raining when he left the bus to walk to Uni where he lectured in Medieval History. As he walked, his mind turned to the question of how he could measure the effects of rain on his clothing, comparing walking and running to work.

Absolution

Neil McGowan

Nineteen eighty-seven. I was ten. It was a year that made headlines for a hundred different reasons; it was the year of lost innocence, when a boy became a man.

My feet bounced along the dusty path. Guns 'n Roses rocked out *Sweet Child of Mine* in my ears. I hummed along to Slash's honeyed guitar tones, imagining myself as a famous rock star. The song was big that summer; everyone was a fan.

Guns 'n Roses gave way to The Bangles and I continued to sing along. Since I'd found it, the path that ran along the bank had been deserted. I can recall the utter certainty of adolescence, that this area was somehow special to me.

Mum and I were visiting her parents. Dad left when I was still a toddler. I knew his face only from pictures.

I didn't question the extended stay; it was the summer break and I was glad to get away from the grime of the city and have wide open spaces to play in. It was a novelty, running through grass and not stepping in something unpleasant left behind by a dog. Later, I came to realise that the move was because Mum lost her job. She was trying to keep us off the streets and the welfare; if that meant swallowing her pride and moving back in with her parents in order to keep me, fine. That summer was a test, I guess, to see how things worked out.

I discovered the path early on. Mum smiled when I told her about it, said I should stay away from the water. I promised I would, and that was the end of it.

I was feeling energetic that day, walking like an Egyptian in time to the music. Brushing sweaty hair out of my eyes, I realized I'd walked further than normal. A copse of trees was just ahead; I figured it would be cool under them. I might even dip my feet in the river, if I found a safe spot on the bank.

Golds and greens gave way to dappled light as I entered the trees. My Walkman faded to silence as side one of the mix tape finished. I walked on, allowing the last section to play on – no point wasting the batteries fast-forwarding to the end.

There was a natural break in the trees. A pair of willows grew close to the bank, branches entwining about eight feet above the ground and forming a natural canopy. I drew closer and sat, leaning against one of the trunks. I popped the cassette out and flipped it over, but didn't press play. The soft gurgle of the river underscored the sweet trill of birds and I relaxed, savouring the moment. My mind conjured idle stories, imagining daring feats carried out by myself. I was a secret agent on the run from the enemy; I was Indiana Jones winning the treasure; I was . . .

There was a boat pulled up on the opposite bank. I wondered if it was old and abandoned for a moment before shaking my head. The paintwork was still bright, the oars neatly shipped.

My imagination kicked up a gear. Was this was part of a real-life mystery? The news bored me; I was more interested in the adventures of the Thundercats, Transformers, and my all-time favourite, the Teenage Mutant Ninja Turtles. Fantasies of solving a crime that foxed the police played out in my head. A bank robbery, perhaps. I could almost hear the applause as I led them to the robbers' secret hideaway.

I smiled: nice daydream; not reality. Yet I was still interested. Why *was* the boat there? Granny hadn't mentioned houses close by; it was one of the things Mum hated – a mile walk to the bus-stop and an hour's journey into town. It was a weekly routine to stock up on food. Granda didn't drive, so Mum was stuck with the walk. I guess she was used to the bustle of the city, where buses ran every few minutes and nowhere was more than a quick bus ride away. Here, a trip lasting an hour in the city needed most of the afternoon.

None of that registered with me; I was just a boy, enjoying wide-open spaces, fresh air and quiet, and being able to play outside without worrying about traffic. I missed few things from the city – leaving my friends was hard; the mixtape in my Walkman was a parting gift from them – but I thought the countryside was fantastic.

I'm nearly forty now, with a wife and child of my own. I look back on that time with fond memories. It was the end of an era for me, a time when innocence fractured.

I leaned forward, gripping a handful of branches to steady myself. I squinted. The trees diffused the sunlight, but enough sparkled on the water to sting my eyes.

In the distance, I could see the shadowed outline of – what? A cabin? Cottage? Maybe a trick of the light, shadows forming in such a way as to give the illusion of a building.

It was impossible to ignore. This had the makings of an adventure. To a boy with an afternoon to kill, it was a fascinating diversion.

First problem: the river. I didn't think it was deep, but I didn't fancy getting soaked. Besides, I thought, if this was an adventure, the water would be teeming with piranhas. Big ones, that would strip my flesh to the bone in under a minute.

No swimming, then. I gripped the branches tighter and leaned further out, looking left. In the gloom, a shadow angled across the water. Bingo! Backing away from the water's edge, I thumbed the Walkman. Starship played *Nothing's Gonna Stop Us Now* as I followed the path deeper into the woods.

A minute's walk and I reached a wooden bridge spanning the river, although 'bridge' was a generous description. A tree trunk, shorn of branches, crossed the water at an angle. A couple of boards were nailed to either side, with a length of rope trailing across to a similar setup at the far side, drooping to less than a foot above the tree in the middle.

I stepped onto the bridge.

It shifted underfoot, just enough to make me catch myself. Arms out to the side, I crossed quickly. Ten seconds and I was on the other side.

The woods seemed different here. Darker, more forbidding. Chewing my bottom lip, I followed the path. Dappled light faded to muted greens and browns as the canopy overhead thickened. No young striplings here; this was the realm of mighty oaks, massive lichen-covered trunks heavy with the weight of years.

Starship finished as I walked, replaced by Cutting Crew. The path was clear of debris and well-trodden; it must lead somewhere, I reckoned.

Soon enough, I spied a ramshackle hut about twenty yards off to the left. I scratched my head, frowning. Who would build a hut in the woods?

I moved closer. The shape began to define itself more clearly. Not a hut, but an old nature hide someone had boarded up. Plastic sheets framed the open viewing ports, an attempt to protect the interior from the elements. Whoever was responsible had been busy: an old door closed the entrance, pieces of wood from an old pallet nailed to the edge so it would fit. More plastic and torn strips of tarpaulin ringed the base. A light flickered inside, a candle I guessed.

Who? The question was foremost in my mind as I crept closer. A tramp, perhaps, creating a safe place to stay during the winter months? I nodded at this, although Mum would have scolded me at the word 'tramp'; I wonder now if this was because she knew how close we were to losing everything.

I was five feet from the door when a muted cry reached my ears, rising in pitch. I stopped the Walkman, strangling the Cutting Crew mid-solo and altered my steps, angling for the window. The last thing I wanted to do was walk in on a couple doing it. I knew vaguely what 'it' was, through schoolyard chats. It sounded like a messy business to me; I was more interested in the latest Thundercats episode.

Still, it must hold some appeal – the seniors looked eager whenever it was mentioned. I got the feeling it was a private act; intruding on a couple's intimacy would be unwelcome.

My face pressed against the grimy plastic; it was translucent at best.

I could see and hear enough. My eyes grew wide. This was no lover's tryst.

He was trying to quiet her. He told her everything was fine; she screamed and swore at him.

"Your fault," she panted. Strands of hair stuck to her forehead. "You said –" her body stiffened and she gave another scream of pain.

He wiped her face. She batted his hands away and swore again.

"Hey, it'll be fine, it'll be okay." Even to me, he wasn't convincing.

"Hah!" She spat to one side. "For you, maybe. My life's ruined." She started to say more, but a fresh contraction of agony gripped her. "Ow, *shiiit!*"

Her body spasmed before relaxing back, a brief respite before the next peak.

I moved to get a better view. A twig snapped underfoot, the crack loud as a gunshot. Heads turned.

"Shit, there's someone out there!" His face was a twisted mask. "Oi you! C'mere!"

He pushed himself to his feet. I saw blood coating his hands and I turned and ran. His footsteps were heavy as he drew closer.

I plunged headlong into the river, ignoring the bridge. I was soaked by the time I made the far shore. I crawled up the bank and staggered to my feet. Cramps bit into my side. In my terror, I was sure he was almost upon me. I risked a glance back.

Nobody there. I squinted across the water. I could just make him out – I think – hidden in the shadows. Watching me.

The rest of the afternoon was anticlimactic. I caught a holy row from Mum for falling in the water. My backside was tender after the skelping she dealt me. It was a few days later that I heard the rest of the story, when Granda came home.

I was supposed to be bed. I couldn't sleep. I was halfway along the landing, thinking about a drink, when I heard Granny's voice from downstairs.

"Hush now! Ye'll wake the boy."

Granda muttered something.

"Aye, but it's no' for his ears, he's too young for that." A creak as she shifted. "Now, tell me what happened."

"It's Davy's lass. They've found her." Granda's voice was grim.

"Not good then?"

I imagined him shaking his head. "No. She was in the woods, about half a mile from here. Poor bugger'd got herself knocked up.

She'd managed to keep it hidden and decided to have the baby in secret with the father's help. They fixed up the old hide."

"Lord!" Another creak. Knowing Granny, she was crossing herself.

"Aye. God only knows what he was going to do afterwards, the silly sod."

"And the lass?" Granny sounded horrified.

"Complications." The word carried a weight of meaning. "Doc said she tore during the delivery and bled to death."

"Dear Lord!" A stifled gasp. "And the father?"

"I'd wager on it being that boy from the farm. They pulled him from the river this afternoon."

I'd heard enough. I crept back to my room, drink forgotten. Sleep was a long time coming that night, and for many nights afterwards. The dead couple plagued my dreams.

I could've helped them. Even now, they are in my prayers every day. I wonder how much they influenced my choices in adulthood. The church helps me, I think, to atone for my mistakes.

It's the baby, you see. All that potential, snuffed out before it had a chance. I've imagined it over the years as a girl. That puts some distance between us; a boy would be too close to me. We lived with my grandparents until Mum found a job that paid enough for us to afford our own place. It was hard, sometimes, but I got a chance in life.

If only I'd found the courage to stay back; if I'd known more about the facts of life. *If, if, if!* Their anger was directed at the hand life dealt them, not me. He wasn't chasing me to hurt me. She needed help; he wanted me to fetch it.

And I ran in terror, leaving her to a lonely, painful end.

The weight of sin lies heavy on me. It's been thirty years now; another thirty might deliver some measure of absolution.

Maybe.

Met Along the Way

Rebecca McKinney

Some people stick in your memory forever, even after the briefest of meetings.

The Man with the Purple Dinosaur

Boulder, Colorado

There was a man who took his purple dinosaur for a walk on the Pearl Street Mall most days, and sometimes he sat in the sun next to the buskers outside the Bookends Café. The dinosaur's neck had been patched with a grubby Band-Aid, and was developing a flop. I sat with my cappuccino and noticed that the dinosaur looked a little more deflated each day. So did the man. Who would he have to talk to, I wondered, when the dinosaur was gone?

Caught Short

Galgate, Lancashire

No matter what you bought, the man in the corner shop in Galgate always made an observation. A couthy presumption or an unwanted intimacy.

If you bought a newspaper, he'd say, "You'll be alright for kindling then."

If you bought pastries, he'd say, "A nice cup of tea and a sticky bun. You're all set up for day."

I bought toilet rolls once, on a Monday morning. He said, "Caught short, were you?"

Wild Bill

Livermore, California

He sat at the corner of the bar and made a bottle of Coors last all night. Strands of colourless hair, oiled back over a face that might have been formed by hand from adobe clay. Years and knowledge worked in by the creator's thumbs. Eyes of slow-burning anthracite. Wild Bill talked so softly you had to be standing right in front of him to hear him. When the bar was quiet, I'd stand there and listen as I dried glasses.

They called him Wild Bill because his Cherokee grandfather worked for Buffalo Bill Cody's Wild West Show. He was an Indian who became a Cowboy. He went to Europe, said Wild Bill. Started a family tradition, you might say. Dad went to Europe too, in '17. I went in '44. He shrugged. We weren't roundin up no doggies then. He shrugged. Blew smoke.

Hey, he said to me one time. You heard of Ishi? Ishi was an Indian, from up Lassen way. They got it real bad, the California Indians. They were too gentle. Didn't like to fight. Ishi was the last Yahi, the last of his tribe. Lived alone in the woods for years. Did you know that? Then he walked out into the white man's world. The anthropologists studied him up good and he died in a museum. There's a book about him, real good book, you should read it.

Wild Bill brought me the book about Ishi and told me to keep it. Said he was moving on. Moving on where, I asked. He shrugged. Said he lived in the car so he could go anywhere. Blew smoke. Finished his Coors. You're a real nice girl, he said. Tipped me a dollar and left. That was the last I ever saw of Wild Bill. I never knew his real name, but I still have his book.

Burger King Parking Lot

Nashville, Tennessee

It had been a long drive down from the high Smokies to Nashville, fuelled by biscuits and gravy and the promise of some hot banjo picking. Dizzied by Nashville's tangled outskirts, we threw down Whoppers and fries in a sticky Burger King. Mine bounced. An old black man sat on a bench at the edge of the parking lot and blinked slowly as he watched me spew my meal onto the tarmac.

Yeah sister, he said, giving me a pendulous shake of the head. Mmm hmm. I *heard* that.

Everyone has a song in Nashville.

Colin

Kentallen, Argyll

We were there to help, but Colin would never ask for it. He would ask for an ear for a story and a bottle of something to take the chill out of his blood. He told us stories of his youth. Travelling the islands, lifting tatties, gathering whelks, selling bits of rags, halting where the view was fine and the folk welcomed your coming. Not like this reservation. How do you like our reservation, he asked. Bet you didn't know we had reservations in Scotland.

The Kentallen Travelling People's Site wasn't anything like a reservation. It was a refrigerated refugee camp for people who once owned the world's room. The trailers and their grim little amenity blocks were tucked up against base of a semi-circular slate rock face. In winter, water cascaded down the north-facing slate wall, wrapping the site in a sheet of ice. This was a place rarely reached by sun or joy.

For something like six months, Colin had been living in half a trailer. He had a seat and a window, and a lot of tarpaulin over the place where his kitchen and bedroom had been. From the top of the rock wall, a slate quarrying company had dropped a boulder onto Colin's roof. He lived to tell the tale because it had happened when he'd gone to town to buy whisky. The quarrying company claimed no responsibility and offered no compensation.

They were just killing him more slowly this way. Colin knew it too. He accepted it the only way he could: with another dram, and the memories of a fine view and a warm welcome.

Ode to the Cliché

Sarah McLean

The pale face of death is as white as snow,
pretty as a picture, with cherry-red lips,
too young to die, though life was not kind,
she was a Cinderella, to tell you the truth.
And honesty is always the best policy,
though the government have a tendency, when making their own,
to forget, and to say things like "change for the better."
Can you mean what you say without saying what you mean?
A rhetorical question: too many needles
in too many haystacks, something like that.
Heartbeats when you look into bright blue eyes:
Forget me not, they say, I'm the next one for you,
I'll be your dream come true, or your worst nightmare.
Two sides to every story, and so many books.
If time is a healer, then those who say magic
does not exist are telling a lie,
with blackened tongues they search for repentance . . .
forgive me father, for I have sinned.
An opening hook, the reader is drawn,
though we know it by heart, we want to know more,
to repeat, to be sure in a hundred ways,
that the sinner pays and the guy gets the girl.
She'll always be nicer than you are yourself,
but she will have flaws, nobody's perfect.
And yet we chase perfection in a vicious circle,
we don't succeed, so we try and try again.

And a circle of course has no beginning,
thus the world is round, no mark from which to start.
We are all equal, on pieces of paper,
and the pen is mightier than the sword.
When a chilling heat settles on the skin,
and the class leave knowing what an oxymoron is,
somewhere in Africa a child is dying,
and we'll put on an advert as it fights for its life.
But adverts are good, they help the economy,
the rich and the poor, in sickness and in health –
tell the couple, I hope you'll be happy together,
but it's always more violent when the man kills the wife.
And the blood-red sunset smears the sky,
like a lipstick stain on a guilty shirt,
and if hurt had heat, it surely would burn,
and if tears could make tracks, then there would be more
pathways to choose from and bulls to grab
by horns tipped with gold, and the devil would say,
If I were in you, I could not be beat out by force,
for violence solves nothing, except when it does.
To climb every mountain and reach for the stars,
we want them, as they will not fall into our lap,
it's unwise to go when the going gets tough,
because things will get better, and you'll miss a trick.
A twist in the tale, a plot unforeseen,
when you sit down to write the next best-seller,
it's best not to start with a description of the rain,
with the sheeting torrents or the tears from the sky.
Why not? If the rain is falling at the start,
do we ignore it? Or do we talk of it, endlessly?
Do we hate the wicked stepmother and feel ourselves intrigued
by the boy in high school with the darkest eyes?

We crave the climax and search for the secret –
they're all deep, but this time, you really mustn't tell.
The key to our hearts can be found in our heads,
or do our heads in fact follow the voices of our hearts?
Our guts join the fray, and we are confused,
do we sink, do we swim, do we bend the rules?
If we know that it works, should we dig down deep,
or will they laugh if we say we have a lump in our throat?
Is a breakup less serious because of the number of fish,
and the sea less a mother because there are now more things?
But if we fly, we are always without wings on our back,
but our hearts can still soar, and hammer, and break.
Avoid the cliché like the plague,
no matter if it fits the bill just right.
But nothing's original, so don't try for that either,
if it's not broke, don't fix it – but if intact, then break it.

Ranald (1895-1918)

LesleyMay Miller

Remembrance is a red poppy,
remembrance is a blue cornflower.

I see my uncle lying on the soil in France,
underneath are seeds of poppies and cornflowers.

His face is still, the agony has gone,
next year others will see the bright cornflowers.

He left his school, his brothers and sisters,
he did not wait for me, I paint the cornflowers.

In the kilt of the Royal Scots he stood straight;
his mother kept that image close; his eyes the colour of cornflowers.

Revealing: First Night at the Writing Club

Malcolm Mitchell

What went on at a writing club? I wasn't really sure.
But playing with words intrigued me – I was captured by the lure.
So I took the chance on an icy night – I jumped into my car,
and then set off to seek out the wordsmiths of Dunbar.

I arrived to seek their secrets, in a world to me uncharted –
but their work was underway before their meeting even started.
I had to get there by seven thirty, and knew I was cutting it fine,
but their habit had already seduced them by seven twenty-nine.

They were keen to go as they set out their aims:
introductions followed, but I forgot the names.
They gave me a picture of some bread and cheese,
and I got ten minutes to write as I pleased.

They laid bare their homework, and looked for critique –
as they searched for advice on their writing technique.
They were high on discussion and mulled over prose,
without a thought of any oral over-dose.

A feminist, Dunbar pirate's viewpoint was depicted,
with the transportation to Australia of those convicted.
Sputum, bile and climate change got some heavy dialogue,
along with cross-dressing and Clifford the Big Red Dog.

Then it was time for me to portray
what I thought about art in my own special way.
My picture of cheese inspired my work
of nightmares, doctors and my dietary quirk.

A good reaction as far as I could tell –
I think they liked it, it went down well.
All my words arranged in lines
were inhaled like tokes in the room's confines.

Nice people was my main thought now –
my initial impression was *very high brow.*
Sonnets and poems that didn't rhyme –
but now they spoke normal and gave me their time.

And then it was over, but how did I feel?
Would their poems entice me to write as surreal?
Probably not, but I will go back –
I'll even give writing poems a crack.

Because my addiction to words is hard to conceal,
and the one thing the word-slingers did reveal
was not so much about author's tricks,
but more about where I could get my fix.

The Making of an Alternative History

Gordon Moodie

It was my grandfather that set our dynasty on the road to greatness. He was the inventor, in the early 21st century, of the '*Ostó Panoiótypo*'. A machine almost forgotten now, but which in its time revolutionised orthopaedic surgery. Although the premise was quite simple – using an MRI scanner attached to (what was really new then) a 3D printer – he could replicate a person's own bones in a hard-wearing resin. In the early days it meant replicating the functioning joint – say the right hip, femur and pelvis – mirror imaging it to make it a left hip and replace the worn out left hip as far as possible with minimum adjustments. Prior to his invention orthopaedic surgery had not advanced much since the time of Admiral Lord Nelson. The flaw was if the "good joint" was also worn or diseased, then no template existed. This is when the real money was made. He had everyone – and I mean everyone – have a full body scan taken when they were in the prime of life so he could hold records of all the potential future arthritic joints and arrange remedial surgery.

There was just too much work for any one man, but the royalties he accrued made Bill Gates' and Rockefeller's earnings combined seem like a pittance. The result was that my father was sent to the best schools and universities to pursue his passion for genetics. The Human Genome Project was in full swing then and Father managed to get a post in the laboratory dealing with the structure and building of bones from DNA. It was the team under his guidance that developed the "Ostó *Taftósimes*" a machine based on Grandfather's "Ostó *Panoiótypo*" but instead of resin this machine re-produced the person's own bones from whatever animal bones were available. The money just kept on rolling in.

Both Grandfather and Father received awards and honours from all over the world, culminating in both receiving the Nobel Prize for Physiology and Medicine. Sadly both died before they could enjoy the acclaim. In turn I too received the best education available and was able to continue in the family's tradition. However I am not interested in prizes – no – my ambition is greater than that. Building on my father's work using his notes and papers, I have constructed a machine that, like my father's '*Ostó Taftósimes*', can make human tissue – only this time making soft tissues: vital organs, blood and brain tissues. By using a person's DNA profile I can recreate them from transformed animal tissue – mostly pigs, the closest match to human tissue. This is so ironic given the creation I am working on. Of course this is only possible as the Americans kept a copy of my subject's DNA all these years ago, which they were forced to give up in the light of the threat made by those insistent gentlemen from al Qaeda to set off a nuclear device in Washington – but at least it means I have the information to resurrect Osama Bin Laden and be remembered for all time as the man who did!

I wonder if anyone ever kept the DNA profile of Adolph Hitler, Uncle Joe Stalin, Pol Pot or even Genghis Khan? Now there would be a challenge . . .

Is That Davey?

Shirley Muir

She hates being jolted awake by the alarm clock.

But wait, that's the telephone screaming in her ear. Her heart pounds in her throat. Heather rolls over and snatches up the phone. The clock tells her it's an ungodly five-thirty. Barely light yet.

"Hello, is Davey there?"

"No," she grunts. "Er, Davey who?"

"Oh, I must have the wrong number. Sorry." The caller hangs up.

Now she's been roused from a deep sleep she waits for her heart rate to subside. Finalising her trip plans online had occupied a good chunk of last evening, till well after midnight in fact. Relief had flooded over her as she clicked the last flight confirmation for an exciting Turkish villa holiday. Her tired body slipped between the sheets knowing the longed-for break was in place, a reward for six months of slog on a challenging market research contract.

Now the results have to be written up and completed, another few days of intense administrative and analytical work. She enjoys the final writing-up phase of these research jobs, where the end is in sight and she is preparing a professional piece of work to present her client.

The phone shrills again.

"Can I speak to Davey?" A man's voice.

"There's no Davey here."

"Who are you then?"

"Who are you?" she says, bristling. "*You* phoned *me*."

"Sorry, it's Davey Bolton I want. I've had an email from him, saying he's stranded in Istanbul and asking for money."

She struggles her body upright, groggy brain stirring into action. With two pillows propping up her back she concentrates her mind and pushes the hair out of her eyes.

"I haven't sent any emails. When?"

"Ten minutes ago. Is Davey there?"

"I don't know any Davey, sorry."

"Oh, I wondered if Davey was all right. Nice guy with a lovely wife. It's a shame what's happened to them. Is he not there?"

"You must have the wrong number."

She hangs up, and then she thinks. Something's happened and this is just the beginning. Less than two minutes elapses and again the phone trills.

"This is Jack from Miller Rental Cars."

"And you've had an email from someone called Davey in Turkey?"

"Yes, I have, and it's worrying me. Is that Kathryn?"

"No, this is Heather Sinclair. My phone number must be on this scam email instead of Davey's. Can you please forward me the email? I don't even know Davey."

"OK, Heather, apologies for the intrusion so early in the morning. I didn't stop to check if this was Davey's genuine phone number. Give me your email address. Just don't click anything in the email. It's poison."

She swings her legs out of bed and stumbles into the office, poking her feet into a pair of slippers and grabbing a dressing gown on the way. Her fingers tremble as she clicks on her Inbox and sees the forwarded message from Jack Miller. She is fearful of opening infected emails but she knows she must. Sure enough her own phone number sits at the bottom of the scam email. Alongside is a tweaked version of what was probably Davey's email address. She reads the note in the message body.

"I'm writing this with tears in my eyes, I had a trip to Istanbul (Turkey) for a short vacation unfortunately I got mugged at the car park of the hotel where I stayed, all cash, credit card and Cell were all stolen from me but luckily for me I still have my passport with me. Please send me money, regards Davey."

To Heather it sounds both naive and unconvincing. Nevertheless the hairs stand up on the back of her neck. Istanbul. She's just booked her own flights.

She Googles this man Davey's correct business number and calls him. It is light now, a decent hour to phone. His number and her number are identical save for one digit. "Are you Davey Bolton? This is Heather Sinclair. My phone number's on a rip-off email saying you are stranded in Turkey."

"Yes," a jaded voice says. "I am so sorry. As you can gather, I'm not in Turkey, only wish I was. Your phone number is like mine, isn't it? 667 instead of 669? I am getting calls every few minutes."

"Well," she says. "I can continue explaining to people phoning me just what's happened to you. They'll be grateful to hear that you're not in real trouble. Would that help?"

"It certainly will. And I was supposed to be starting to fit out Mr Patel's pharmacy premises today. But now I'll have to stay here with my IT specialist and decontaminate the laptop and reset my email accounts. It will take me the rest of the day to apologise to all my customers."

"I'm so sorry this has happened to you, Davey. I'm only glad I can do something to assist," Heather said.

"Thank you, that's very kind," he says, his voice shaky. "Losing this work will cost me best part of five grand, so there'll be no holidays for us in a long while. And Istanbul is definitely top of my bucket list. What a coincidence. It almost made me laugh."

Heather thinks he sounds close to tears.

Armed with a cup of coffee and a notebook to take details of the phone enquiries for Davey, she concludes that she won't make a start on the last section of the research project today. She fully expects the phone to keep ringing every few minutes. But she doesn't mind if her day can be usefully spent sorting out Davey's difficulty.

Several local business contacts ring her during the morning and she chats to them about Davey, whom she had never heard of until dawn today. High quality joinery work from Davey is the common denominator. He certainly comes across as a competent and skilled tradesman.

And they all ask after his wife, Kathryn.

Mid-morning, the local church minister, Andrew calls. "Hello Andrew, have you had this scam email from Davey Bolton, too?"

"I have. We are customers of his. Davey carried out a piece of fantastic restoration work for the church choir. He was very proud of it and didn't even bill us."

The Reverend Andrew expresses concern for Davey. He knows that he and his wife are under severe strain due to her recent illness. It has caused Davey to lose a lot of days off work and Andrew worries that their finances may be under pressure.

"Davey doesn't need this kind of setback right now," he says. "I'll pop round later and see Kathryn. I married them in St Margaret's only last year; it was an enchanting wedding."

"Oh Andrew, that is so sad. I have never met Davey but I have been overwhelmed by the outpouring of support I have listened to today. The people who have phoned me obviously like and respect Davey."

"Yes, Davey's a perfectionist and his work diary is always full," Andrew says. "You can't fault his excellence or dedication, and his optimism is generally unwavering. In fact, they are a delightful couple. When you see them together it's apparent that Kathryn is the love of his life. She's a real treasure."

Heather is shocked to hear in the ensuing phone conversations that most of Davey's contacts – from his compromised email list – actually believe he's stranded in a Turkish police station.

Until this morning she reckoned she herself could spot a spoof email a mile away. Now she's not so sure that others can when they know and care about the victim involved. It seems to cloud their judgement. But she understands perfectly why that would be, and why people today want to check whether Davey does in fact need assistance.

Callers continue to suggest ways they might lend a hand to Davey and Kathryn to see them through this crisis. *Does Davey need money? Can I send a cheque to his wife? Does he want flights back home? I'd like to meet him at the airport.* Offers stream in.

One woman divulges to Heather that Kathryn has recently suffered quite a late miscarriage and it has affected them badly. She even volunteers to visit Davey's mum and reassure her that Davey and Kathryn are both all right and this is just an unfortunate computer scam.

A call from the pharmacist comes through. "I'm sorry but I've just had this email from Davey. Is he OK? I know he called to say he wanted to delay the work on my new shop for a day, and that's not going to inconvenience me at all. Suits me better, in fact. Now, is there anything I can do to help?"

Heather is relieved on behalf of Davey that at least one thing is turning out well today. He will be reassured to have his important shopfitting job to start on tomorrow, instead of bemoaning the loss of an important source of income.

The pharmacist is another customer of Davey's who marvels at his skills and professionalism. "Sorry to have troubled you," he says, "I bet you've had a busy day unravelling Davey's unwanted email muddles. Well done you."

She smiles to herself and rings Andrew back.

"Andrew, can you help me with something, please?"

By evening the calls have faded to a trickle. It's been a rollercoaster of a day, and now it's done. Her research project has lain untouched but she can tackle it tomorrow. A day away from it will do both her and the report good. She will look at it with fresh eyes in the morning.

After a long and interesting day she finally climbs into bed.

A fortnight later the market research assignment is bound and has been submitted to her client. Her invoice is in the post on the way to the client. Heather boards the plane to Istanbul. She stows her coat, takes her window seat and fastens her seatbelt. Heather wears a smile as she gazes out of the window at the bright blue of the sky. This much-needed break will refresh her mentally and physically now that the six-month intensive work stint has concluded. And the very welcome client fee will be in her bank account when she returns. Her destination is a rented villa an hour's taxi ride from Istanbul airport. Sunshine, swimming pool, reading and relaxation beckon. Bliss.

A slim man with shoulder muscles outlined through his shirt stops at her seat row. He shoves a chunky holdall into the overhead locker above her head as if it were weightless. As he slides into the aisle seat, a woman sits down next to Heather in the middle seat. The couple retrieve their respective seatbelt halves and connect them with simultaneous metallic clinks.

Heather turns to her neighbour, extending her hand.

"Hello," she says. "I'm Heather."

"Hello," the woman says, taking her hand and offering a soft smile. The woman's fingers are freezing despite the warmth of the plane and the lovely summer sunshine outside.

"I'm Kathryn Bolton and this is my husband Davey." She lays her hand on his knee and her smile displays straight, pearly-white teeth. Her pale, thin face glows with pleasure.

Heather warms to this young woman.

"I'm so excited," the woman says to Heather with an air of confidentiality. "We won this holiday in a raffle at the church, which we didn't even remember buying tickets for, did we Davey?"

"We didn't, love, and that's a fact."

His face lights up as he clasps her delicate hand in his, like a precious jewel. As they gaze at one another Heather watches his eyes. They sparkle with love. He strokes his wife's hand as if it were rich velvet.

Heather counts herself blessed to have finally met this charming couple face to face. She feels for a moment like an intruder in their private bubble.

Kathryn turns to Heather and murmurs, with a giggle, "We're having a second honeymoon, really."

Don't Look Now

Jane Patmore

Supernatural, ghost stories, horror – they've never been my favourite genre, neither in books nor film. I think it's because I know that the stories are not true so I can't engage with them fully. Also, my over-active imagination means that after watching a scary film or reading a book which is full of suspense I find myself horribly spooked, jumping at the noise of the wind and catching glimpses of shadowy beings around me. However, I had to make an unexpected train journey and my friend Sheila lent me a book for the trip. It was quite a good read actually, although some of the scenes of the gruesome murder in a car were described far too vividly for my liking.

It had been a couple of weeks since I'd completed the book and the plot was fading quickly from my memory, but there was something about that Tuesday night which brought the tale to mind again. The setting had all the hallmarks of a classic horror story – a dark night, wild gusts of wind, driving rain, low cloud and a near-empty multi-story car park. As I walked across the stark concrete towards my car, my footsteps echoed around the hallways, speeding up and almost keeping pace with my heartbeat. I was feeling more and more nervous – anyone, or anything, could be lurking here – and when I reached my car I leapt in and quickly pressed the central locking button to secure my safety from the unseen, imaginary terrors.

The adrenaline in my body had the effect of heightening all my senses. I was sure I could smell something unusual, a bit like stale cigarette smoke or maybe something weirdly metallic, and my hands were shaking a little as I turned the key in the ignition and switched on the headlights. My coat was wet, it was a struggle for the fan to keep up with the damp air and the windscreen was steaming up. I turned on the air conditioning and at rubbed the glass with my gloved hand, but not before I saw the imperceptible shape of words forming on the window: "Don't look behind you..."

Of course, it wasn't actually those words in full, there certainly wasn't a letter 'D' at the front, I could only read the first letter of the final word, and I'd wiped my hand across it almost before the writing had registered at all. I couldn't be certain that I hadn't imagined the whole scenario, and I was starting to feel cross at myself for letting my thoughts run out of control.

I drove home as quickly as I could and was reassured to see familiar lights shining out across the farmyard as I parked the car. I closed the front door behind me and leant against it, relieved to be out of the stormy weather and back in the warmth of my house. Except that the house didn't feel quite as warm as usual. Not exactly cold, but as though a window was ajar somewhere. I dumped my keys on the hall table and called out to Derek, ready to chastise him a little for forgetting to secure the house, or for wasting electricity. However, my husband didn't answer. He wasn't in the kitchen, or the living room. I ran upstairs but all the bedrooms were in darkness, and the bathroom door was open, so he wasn't in there. Returning downstairs, I glanced at my phone but there was no message from Derek and he'd not left a note in the customary place in the kitchen.

My levels of anxiety rocketed, and I was both perplexed and thoroughly pissed off that Derek was not at home. As I walked through the silent living room, I once again caught an indiscernible scent of cigarette smoke and that strange metallic smell also. Oh for goodness sake, I thought to myself, now I was having olfactory hallucinations! Enough was enough, and I picked up my phone to call my friend Sheila. I stared in panic at the blank unlit screen, but thankfully a couple of jabs brought it back to life – it would have been one cliché too far to be alone in the dark without a phone.

Sheila answered my call and sensing the hysteria in my voice she agreed immediately to drive round and pick me up. Their car arrived within a few minutes, Stuart at the wheel, Sheila in the passenger, seat and even before she'd knocked at the door I was outside and hastening towards the vehicle. "This is all your fault," I said, as her husband turned the car around and started to drive us away, "You should not have let me borrow that ghost story."

As we turned out of the farmyard, Stuart's headlights swept across my car where I'd abandoned it. The windows had steamed up again, and this time I could read the words written on the windscreen: "Don't look behind your sofa . . ."

Is This What it Takes?

Eric Platten

We have all seen the pictures, the
biggest mass migration of refugees
since World War 2.
Overcrowded boats, if that's what they
can be called, arriving on beaches and
overwhelming small islands. People hoping
for a piece of paper that will give them
some status.

All agree that something must be done.
But no one can agree on what that should
be. Because it's happening elsewhere, politicians
say it's not up to us, we can't take any more.
Stop them at source, arrest the traffickers who
take the money and cause all this misery. Destroy
the boats so no more can be cast adrift to see where
the tides will take them.

But then a lorry is parked, no fresh air and people
crammed inside, to suffocate and putrify in the heat,
at the side of the road. We thought that was bad, but
worse was to come. Have we seen the image that will
finally make people sit up, take notice, stop and say
no enough is enough, we have to do more.
Or do we wait for more 3 year old children to be
washed up, dead on the seashore?

The Sale

Jules A Riley

"Magnificent barns like this were built by the Dutch in the seventeenth century."

"It's *that* old, Mister Whitty?"

"No sir, but coming on a hundred years."

"It sure is, as you say, a magnificent structure," Jeremiah Grudge scribbled notes on his clipboard pad. "It will be taken into consideration".

"You don't get mortised and tenoned pegged beams like that anymore. A carpenter using a handful of tools, none of them fancy."

"All will be considered Mister Whitty."

"You tell your prospective buyers this ain't cheap. Those solid beams came from matured wood. Last *another* hundred years, maybe more."

"I see there ain't windows?"

"No need. You open up to plenty of sunlight. Enough to see what you're doing and plenty of hours to do it in.

"No power either?"

"Never saw the reason. See how them beams are finished, rounded off? That's craftsmanship. If you get the chance to touch them you'll feel how smooth they are, just as smooth as the day they were finished."

"I don't doubt how good this barn is, Mister Whitty. You have to understand it'll be part of a package on auction day."

"Is that all this homestead is, just a package on auction day?"

"We all have to live with the times."

"Live with the times? The Baileys at Maynard Creek got nothing near what their place was worth."

"Kept them straight, Mister Whitty."

"Heard Nathan Bailey couldn't find work anywhere in the state."

"Some do, some don't. They reckon he moved to Chicago."

"I'm just in my forties, Mister Grudge. I was born a farmer. Don't reckon I could live in a city."

"I know it's hard to take. None of us asked for this *Depression* as they call it. All due to greed if you ask me. Some city folk have got a lot of answers to give."

"You'll be doing fine?"

"Nothing is as good as it was."

"They can take it all. I can't fight this anymore."

"Sorry it's come to this. I'll get back to you. Give you some idea, but you have to understand it'll depend on the day."

Adam Whitty watched as Jeremiah Grudge drove away, stirring a cloud of dust. Adam walked into the barn and slumped on a crate then rummaged in the inside pocket of his frayed jacket and pulled out a crumpled and faded photograph. It was the image of a family taken some time not long after the start of the century, an era where everyone having their photo taken had to stay stock still. The subjects all looked nervous and unsmiling except for the young boy sat cross-legged at the front of the group whose face was full of laughter. A tear dropped onto the photograph and Adam wiped at his runneled face and then smudged the photograph against his jacket sleeve. He thought of that young boy who'd grown into a man and like so many brave young men, more than a decade past, had left their homes to serve their country. He wondered how they would have reacted to what was happening to the world they left behind.

Strolling out of the barn Adam Whitty watched as the last rays of sunshine streamed into the cathedral space, before pulling the doors shut. On his return to the clapboard house where he had been born and his father before him, he kicked at the parched earth again and again, then slumped on the stoop to gaze over the land that soon would be his no more.

Taid's Magic Lines

Keith Saunders

(taid: North Wales name for grandfather)

"Go to the 'old wash-house' – your Taid's only just started," said his mother.

The boy was puzzled. What would Taid be doing in the 'old wash-house'? He could not remember the last time his grandfather went there. Only he went to the old building across the yard.

There was a routine of daily action replays. The boy would lean against the peeling brown paint door then lift his bicycle up over the high step. As he pushed it across the flagstone floor, there was always the reassuring 'click-click' of well-oiled wheel bearings amplified by the bare walls and high slate roof. The bicycle was always left propped against a wooden stand near to the old disused copper boiler that gave the outhouse its name. This oak post; about three feet high with spoke-shaved edges that had smoothed with time, and with a patina splattering of paint and oil stains, was supported by a wide, heavy, cruciform base. A strong metal peg protruded horizontally from near the top of the post.

The routine completed, the boy would leave. Only once did he really explore the shelves groaning with jam jars and biscuit tins from Harlech Castle and Llandudno Pier, full of nuts, bolts, screws and nails that had gone rusty waiting for the day when they would be useful. But, amongst all this, there was something different. At the very end of the top shelf there was an old half-pound St Bruno tobacco tin: rectangular; with rounded corners, a hinged lid and a triangle of ventilation holes at either end.

The boy had opened the lid. The inside of the tin was packed with grease – there were things embalmed inside that looked like tiny fishing floats. He had dug a fingernail into the grease, lifted out a short handle and held it to the light: extending from this swan quill were fine bristles, as long as his hand. He meant to ask what they were for . . . but he never did.

Go to the 'old wash-house' – your Taid's only just started.

The door was partly open: the boy pushed against the peeling brown paint, stepped onto the flagstone floor, then stopped – transfixed. Instead of the usual monochrome, the room was lit up by a huge circle of spinning yellow.

He moved forward very slowly.

The strong metal peg near the top of the old oak post was protruding through the axle boss of a large, fresh yellow painted, cartwheel. The yellow spokes were flickering into each other because the wheel was turning.

The old man sat, with his back to the boy, to one side of the wheel. He did not speak, though he must have heard the boy's gasp of surprise. As the boy was watching, a black line appeared – as if by magic – on the yellow side of the wheel. The boy stepped closer. His grandfather then lifted another quill handle from the selection in the jar by his feet, and pulled the long bristles through his pinched finger and thumb. Crystals of turpentine dripped onto the stone floor. He dipped the brush into one of the open paint pots, then lifting the brush to the still turning wheel, and with a hand and eye as steady as death, he made a perfect red line, right around the wheel, just a little above the black one.

The boy had never seen his Taid 'line' a wheel before . . . and he never did again.

Go to the 'old wash-house' – your Taid's only just started.

"What happened to Taid's old lining brushes?" the middle-aged man asked his mother.

"I don't know. Why?"

The man was silent because there was a flicker of that old Celtic self-doubt and melancholy as he had thought of his own life.

His Taid could do it – he'd seen him.

But, had he ever made Magic Lines on Spinning Yellow Wheels?

What the Shore Said

Anne Shivas

I screech, am steep cliff, surging water,
strand, dune and marram grass,
shell and bone hollow, rolled to sand,
spume, white horses' manes on surf,
gannet guzzling mackerel; am blood
anemone, buckies, bladderwrack, kelp,
thrum of a guitar. Upturned empty
crab, blue volcanic scooped out rock,
oyster catcher cooried doon on one leg,
I am crow, hopping. Herring gull, I sail
close to the wind, am sea pink, pink weed,
am snow-strewn, ice sheets cracked,
am an eye, wide open, rooted, children's voices,
fire and song, bud, wee shoals o fish
in slips o waves, broad and flat.
I didn't know un-seeable nets
flip-flops, rose hip, wellie boots,
could be woven around me,
flounder and dog, t-shirts, cagoules.
Salt, gusty, calm, raging, I didn't know
the gods would haul me, dolphin,
porpoise, killer whale, krill back,
pull us in by our dreams.

Being Mrs Smith *(excerpt)*

Cheryl Smith

Mr Smith has been given a shocking diagnosis and little real hope of recovery, so, hand-in-hand with Mrs Smith, he has embarked on a quest for healing. Drawn to the ancient teachings and traditional medicines of the Amazon, the Smiths arrive in South America and prepare to meet the healers who offer hope that was nowhere to be found in the Western world.

Part 2 Ch. 1 Follow the Brown Dirt Road 22-23 April 2014

The Peru that Mr Smith wanted to visit is a diverse and magical place full of hot springs, dense jungles, beautiful cities and sacred sites. Pucallpa has none of those things. Pucallpa is dusty, dirty and primitive, and it was our new home.

These small absences were of no matter though; we weren't there to admire the views. We could do the tourist trail later, if there was anything left in the budget at the end of it all. For now, we were relieved to have come this far, and we were looking forward to the next chapter with excitement and optimism and trepidation.

Our host Silvia met us at the airport. A well-travelled Italian who had settled in Peru and made it her business to develop an intimate knowledge of the local shamanic scene, she had assured us that the best practitioners of ancient medicines were from this part of the country. There were now countless treatment centres in more exotic locations like the Sacred Valley to the south and Iquitos to the north, but, she told us, their best shamans were recruited mainly from Shipibo families from around Pucallpa. The Shipibo-Conibo tribespeople have an unbroken lineage in the ancient art of curanderismo, or traditional healing, and their services are highly desired among North American and European spiritual seekers. In response to this modern demand, many of them are now focused on business, and some of them can and do command alarmingly big bucks.

We would have access to the same, or maybe even higher, standards of expertise but without the hefty price tag. We would be focused purely on caring for Mr Smith while the healers did their job of getting him better. And yes, it could be done. It would take as long as it would take but Silvia had seen miracles performed by the very people we'd be meeting in the coming days. She herself had been close to death when she'd arrived four years earlier.

She introduced us to members of the team she had gathered for us: her niece Luisa, who had been hired to cook and clean, and Emilio, a local man who would provide transport in his mototaxi – a motorbike with a rickshaw attached, the most common mode of transport in Pucallpa. We were attracted to the novelty of that, and a bit disappointed to be taken to our hotel by people carrier along with several other weary travellers. We wouldn't miss out though– in the weeks to come there would be plenty of opportunity to enjoy the unique and dubious pleasures of dust in our eyes, grime on our clothes and zero vehicle suspension. Meantime, the warmth in the welcome assured us that we were in the company of like minds and sympathetic hearts.

As we drove along, taking in the otherness of the environment, I wondered whether I could get used to the heat. It was 10pm and had been dark for five hours but it was still as hot as my northern blood could endure. Mr Smith had travelled more widely than I had and could adapt, and yes, so could I. I'd come this far with him and I'd do whatever was necessary to see it through.

At the beginning at least, we did feel a bit like tourists. We were spending the night in the hotel because our new home was on a lagoon on the Ucayali River, a tributary of the Amazon, and at this time of year the dirt tracks were under water, with the only access by boat. Our hosts had shown up to meet us wearing boots and bearing a large oar apiece; they were going to find their own way home in the darkness of the night. They would come back in the morning to escort us via one of the local motorboats for hire.

Meantime, Silvia flirted with Mr Smith, and Mr Smith, charmingly to my eye, didn't notice that he was being flirted with. He would be in the care of four beautiful women, she said (there was a second domestic supporter waiting at home), and would want for nothing in the way of feminine comfort and attention. That would provide the basis of care that he needed while the curanderos concentrated on his healing.

She had arranged for us to stay in the best room in the hotel, the one that proudly boasted a Jacuzzi and a mini-bar. It would be a shame to waste them: we were only staying for one night and we had been warned that, although every effort was being made for us, the standards of comfort in the average Peruvian home were different. So, spent as we were from a journey of over twenty-four hours, we sank into the bubbles together and shared a modest bottle of beer. This would be our last taste of luxury for a long time, and we savoured it.

* * *

Our first mototaxi ride, to the lagoon, was short, sticky and grimy. In daylight, the town was not pretty, but it did have colour going for it. It reminded me of Mr Smith's remark the previous day. On the flight from Amsterdam to Lima, he'd gestured out of the window to the Andes below, grinned like only he could grin, and said,

"We're not in Scotland anymore, Toto . . ."

We surely weren't. Just like Toto and Dorothy, we were in a strange land of garish colours that clashed, with each other and sometimes with us. It was a land of brashness and noise. This was the land in which, like Toto and Dorothy, we would encounter strange beings and stranger challenges. We would face our fears head-on and reveal ourselves to be stronger than we knew.

This was the land from which we would find our way home.

First, there was the yellow brick road to follow. Though in our case, it began with more of a brown dirt road and what looked like a browner and dirtier river.

Boarding the boat with its makeshift canopies of discarded sheets of plastic and its weathered wooden benches, we were beginning to see the reality of what we'd been told to expect. Standards were different here, and though our new home was considered luxurious – it boasted running water, electricity and a flush toilet – it wouldn't be what we were used to. That was okay, we told ourselves, because when your only focus is to get a job done, your surroundings tend to blur into invisibility. Anyway, how bad could it be?

At first sight, worse than expected. In the novel heat, we were just beginning to relax into the journey, trailing our fingers in the cool water and thinking what a shame that those derelict wooden shacks along the shore were spoiling the view, when the boatman steered towards, then moored alongside, the most precarious-looking of them.

It was a wonder, this house, in that it was still standing. High above the lagoon, propped up on stilts that looked suspiciously rotten, its balcony overhung the water. Beneath it, baling out a rowing boat, was a wild woman, a lean, powerful and earthy Amazonian goddess with a smile as big as her heart would turn out to be. This was our first sighting of Claudia, the Columbian ayahuasquera who would be our domestic support, nurse and holder of ceremonial space.

As we climbed the steps at the back of the house, they warned us against using the fenced porch that ran the length of the building. It was overdue for repair and the rotting wood could give way under our weight. We weren't tempted to take the risk; the old, stained, bright green porcelain toilet, rust-ridden barbecue and other assorted detritus weren't exactly beckoning us.

The interior was contrastingly agreeable though, and the goddesses' efforts for our comfort were apparent in the room they had prepared for us. For privacy, the window to the kitchen and main living area had been covered with the traditional Shipibo embroidery that was to become familiar. The glassless windows were covered in mosquito mesh and makeshift plastic blinds installed against the worst of the storms that had been troublesome lately. This room was small and basic but it was not uncomfortable really, if we could lay aside our usual expectations – and of course we could, in appreciation that things were different here. Things were different but this was real hospitality and we were glad of it. Our hearts did sink slightly at the sight of the twin beds but we could always push them together, and that small disappointment was overshadowed by our blossoming gratitude.

The house generally reminded me of the scenes in the old Doris Day film Calamity Jane, where Jane is joined in her log cabin by the frilly and feminine actress and suddenly the place is transformed with flowers and pretty curtains. This was certainly a run-down wooden structure, but it was a richly decorated run-down wooden structure. In this case, rather than gingham and roses, the adornments were the accoutrements of the ayahuasquera. Intricate Shipibo wall-hangings, strings of beads and feathers, sticks of Palo Santo and bottles of Agua de Florida; tools of the shaman's trade served the additional purpose of creating a welcoming atmosphere.

Something that alarmed us both at first was that everybody was smoking. We were no longer used to this, and we were dismayed at the incongruity of a place of healing infused with cigarette smoke. We'd heard of mapacho, the pure tobacco used by shamans as a sacred medicine, but we didn't know much about it. We were reassured when they told us, and we quickly found out for ourselves that these cigarettes are clean, odour-free and very different to the nicotine varieties that so repelled us. Over the coming weeks, we lifelong non-smokers would even have a few puffs ourselves in the context of ayahuasca ceremonies. Our commitment to healthful recovery was opening our minds and increasing our willingness to engage in whatever practices were in harmony with the treatments we had come here for.

The same principle applied to food: we would act on local advice about what would work best both with Mr Smith's constitution and with the medicines. Our research and our own limited experience had taught us that diet is a crucial component of a shamanic healing process, and in any case we were in no position to insist on our own regime. The new diet was to begin immediately, and in the early afternoon we were introduced to Claudia's culinary skills and Silvia's nutritional standards. It hardly surprised us that these differed from ours, but we were surprised by the apparent over-use of sugar, vegetable oils and refined salt. But Silvia's careful attentiveness to our individual needs impressed us and we were willing to un-learn everything we knew about eating for health. We'd been resigned to bland food and restricted intake, so the tasty and abundant lunch was an unexpected pleasure, and we were ready to embrace the whole package; we would put aside some of our own ideas of what was healthy and we'd accede to the experts and to the wisdom of the plants themselves.

In the ceremony room, a recess that led from the dining area and opened out onto the balcony over the river, half a dozen mattresses were laid out and covered with patterned blankets. A plastic mesh hammock hung above them and various pipes and bowls lay half-hidden in corners. I baulked slightly at the animal skin on the floor, and I never did get used to touching it, but the when-in-Rome attitude prevailed regardless. In the coming days we would be introduced to some of the indigenous healers who would be working with us in this space, which would also serve as a living area, reading nook and treatment room.

For now though, exhausted by the newness of everything, including the strange novelty of having no responsibilities for a while, we pushed the single beds together, erected our double mosquito net over and around them, and slept deeply, entwined beneath the gaudy blankets.

Cockenzie Power Station

Jock Stein

1 Farewell to the Lums o' Cockenny

Grey and white across the sky
fly shrouds and cirrus clouds;
above the Firth, the Fife hills flit
from west to east, and brush
a laid back, painterly horizon;
shore lines match this movement,
picture framing work and living space.

The vertical begins far down, where
hidden shafts lift coal from underground
to make a profit out of power.
Two chimney stacks take over, bound
up and away, cock a Cockenzie snook
at flat earth thinking, lift our hearts,
change landmarks to blue sky marks.

Sailors set their homeward way by them,
golfers guide their forward play by them ,
locals spend their every day by them –
but not for long. Already, pylons hang
their empty cables in a sad catenary,
without a whimper, let alone a bang.
The universe tomorrow's horizontal.

2 Waiting for the End

Four ghostly hoppers face the concrete
music of demolition, sitting upright,
aghast, like dogs on death row, linked
by frozen metal leads, sad skeleton
of Scottish Power.

No, this is not a post-referendum poem,
just a header through the empty space,

without the chimneys for two goal posts.
A ball of words could skiff half o'er
to Aberdour,

and sink the workplace memories
respectfully within the Firth of Forth.
Soon the levelled landscape will
shrug off its past, and host an outcome
sweet or sour.

3 Boxing Day 2015

This empty box has folded – its time and space
exploded, christmas past, new year no' here
yet. Yet what?

Exit stage left, braw bygone social age,
your rage expired with Scargill and McGahey.
Wait. For what?

We live on private festival left overs,
meat digested, leaving us in flesh and
bone somewhat

confused, dry, knowing that the feast
has left a debt, but how can we afford
to run what

ought to be a welfare state, now saddled,
bridled with demolishing austerity, to
pull down what

we built with hope, a level playing field
of health and education for a kinder world.
So, now what?

Gap site, dusted down, for someone fly
enough to seize the day and fly a kite
to save what

should be our own foreshore, not the private
land of strange investors? Who and how and
why and what

are public questions. After Boxing Day
the local people want their say.

November Blues

Cynthia Stephens

November blue and orange, breakers white
as horses on the sand where paths collide,
and hoof marks trace the arc of luck, and love
is in the wind of this dear beach. I reach
the edge, where water roaring high on waves
bears down and on along the sand. The neighs
of distant animals are lost as drops
of rain mix with the spray, soft on my face.
Yet in the space between the waters sound
I hear in dreams the swimmers, voices found
from deep beneath the ocean; fishes' tails
like mermaids, waving, welcoming. These gales
are glorious, they claim us, own us, now.
Forever, bright November, or January white.

Cloud Villanelle

Diana Stevens

I linger alone watching clouds drift by,
touching a void of starflower blue,
spiral up, up to where shape-shifters fly.

Herbal tang, light as air, less than a sigh.
Skirl of cricket, drone of bee, passing through,
to where I lie and watch clouds drifting by,

like a circus parade, waving goodbye.
Twist and twirl, swirl, follow the thermals to
spiral on up to where shape-shifters fly.

The upside-down people who soar too high
are deposed, dissipate and rise anew,
spiralling up to where shape-shifters fly.

I gaze, undisturbed in the heat of July
as snapping dragons spot prey to pursue
which spirals up to where shape-shifters fly.

Here for a moment, the blink of an eye,
the dragons no more, dissolved in the blue.
I shall linger now to watch clouds drift by
spiralling up to where shape-shifters fly.

Circumstances

Judith Stewart

Thanks very much, he says
as he slides my coin
from polystyrene cup to pocket.
A pound means a lot tae me.

I ask the obvious question –
how come he's sitting in the rain
in a sleeping bag? He shrugs.

Just circumstances, family stuff
– maistly ma ain stupidity.

Then I ask how he feels
that the best sites on Princes Street
are taken by people from elsewhere:
Roma, East Europeans, Kurds . . .

so he gives me a short talk
on the global economy:
capitalism, corruption and bankers.

Ah dinnae resent thae migrants
he says. *We're aw the same*
– they're my brothers.
And I like this sad young man
with his bad teeth and generous heart.

As I move on up the Playfair Steps
he calls after me, *Thanks, pal.*
Ah'll dae the same fur you some day.

Cultures Clash and Invent Rituals

Sheila Thacker

It started well enough: we had been gathering in numbers over the last few days, being made welcome by locals and expats who had made this small island their home. Like Jane they were there to re-invent themselves and live happy lives, only they bought their baggage intact: fragile, explosive, handle with care, damaged goods, written all over them in invisible ink. A motley crew indeed!

My sister Jane died when she was 52 years old. She had been living in Syros for six years, had gone to find herself and write a best-seller which never appeared, but the bottles of Retsina were prolific! She taught English in a friend's school where she was known as *Meessis Yane.* She was always ready with a supply of stories to tell about her students, along with her bitingly funny observations about her fellow expats (she would never admit to being one of them). She became vicious and not funny and she moved from being a complex intellectual to a remote plane where she was the only person she could relate to.

When she was playing *A Hitch Hiker's Guide to the Galaxy* on her 'new' Amstrad or parodying twee expats at supper parties she made everyone laugh, but always with an edge to it – hoping they would not be the next butt.

Eventually her liver failed and she spent her last six weeks in the Island Hospital, on the 3rd floor – significant, because local superstition said people never came off the 3rd floor vertically.

On April 20th 1997 at 4pm, she died. According to Greek law she was buried the next day in the Greek Orthodox cemetery. They were less than impressed at having to house her (not only British but an atheist to boot) but agreed, as in three years her remains would be exhumed and taken to the Ossuary – as is customary in Greece – or "that bloody potting shed," as Jane had referred to it.

She had always said she wanted to be buried in the British graveyard, which was next door to the Orthodox Church. So instead of the Ossuary, we arranged for a reburial. However, we hadn't allowed for all things Greek being terribly complicated. No one had been buried there since 1965 as it was deemed full. Eventually, after three years of administrative negotiations, the Consulate agreed they would find room for a new and much-diminished burial.

So it happened. No one ever imagined it like this. Friday 2nd June was the exhumation, not customary for relatives to witness; they have a ceremony when the bones are taken to the Ossuary. However, the grave digger had lost Jane's name plate and so asked for a relative to identify her. This task was performed by her daughter; a Greek friend went with her, expecting her to collapse in hysterics. However we are British; reserved and stiff upper lipped. "Oh yes," she said, "that's her alright, I can see as clearly as if there were flesh on her brow . . . I would recognise that scowl anywhere!"

She then had to do various deals. The gravedigger would arrange for a 'nice box' for the remains – in exchange for many Drachmas – and the Priest would organise a certificate of hygiene which would allow the reburial. More Drachmas – she had now been relieved of the equivalent of £400! We were rapidly discovering when dealing with Greek bureaucracy, accepting it in its entirety without question is the only way forward!

Assuming all was organised, we arrived just before 4 pm on the allotted day; Tuesday 6th June 2000, under a baking sun and clear blue sky. We were bemused by the lack of a grave, gravedigger and of course the all important expensive box. In a small shed-like office attached to the Orthodox Church, we learned that the original gravedigger, and the box, were both missing – the said gentleman, being on holiday, had taken the box and Drachmas with him, or at least omitted to provide the box before departure! Jane meantime was in a tin box on a shelf-cum-table.

"He is cheeky man!" declared an on-duty grave digger.

"A thief," I'd have said.

The grave digger said "ah," as inspiration struck, and produced a laundry bag into which Jane was quickly transferred. Two arms, check: two legs, one torso and one skull all present and correct! We had one of those 'did that really happen?' moments, as he threw said bag over his shoulder and picked up a pickaxe.

"Come," he commanded.

Two others with spades walked with him whilst we followed. Had he sung "Hi Ho, Hi Ho" we would, like the seven dwarfs, have joined in without question! This is what shell shock does to people.

The motley crew joined us in the short walk to the British Cemetery, someone saying how Jane would find this hilarious and hoot with laughter.

All I could think during this procession was: 'poetic justice.' Some years earlier Jane had had my Mother's ashes posted to her in a jiffy bag!

She was marched up the street in the laundry bag, which the grave digger was now swinging, and then plonked down against a tree whilst the three grave diggers hacked the hard-baked earth, untouched for over 35 years in the blistering heat.

A nightmare! An American woman wailed, "Nico said I should not have come, he knows how emotional I am, this is awful, this is not what I expected, oh, Nico was right, he knows I am so emotional!"

I looked at a resting spade and wondered, if I batted her in the mouth would that be assault in Greece? I decided it probably would be, so best not!

Another was repeating, "This isn't our culture; the Greeks should realise and be more sensitive and understanding."

It was nobody's culture, we made it up as we went along!

The grave was now deemed ready, and the bag lifted and dropped unceremoniously into its hopefully-final resting place. I threw a flower onto the bag and others followed, the diggers said some Greek prayers, drank water from plastic bottles, then started to heap earth back into the grave. When half filled a watering can was produced and water was liberally sprayed on their handy-work! I felt my shoulders twitch, then tried in vain to suppress the strangled giggles rising in my throat. I had to walk away, imagining my sister unfurling like a ballet dancer in *Swan Lake*. I tried to explain to my husband that pure hysteria had set in, not tears. Mrs American now saw me as a kindred spirit.

With the task completed and flowers laid on top of a normal looking grave, a friend of Jane's had volunteered to make a speech. He talked of his own feelings and emotions: passing the hospital always brought a lump to his throat.

I started to say something, but was swiftly interrupted by a Dutch woman who threw her arms around my neck, exhaling breath and sobbing: that she was *so empty*.

She meant that the bottle was empty, and she was decidedly fu'! She loved Jane, she was her best friend and she had lost two more friends in the last three years she could not talk, she was *so empty*. We wished!

"Your sister knew exactly what she was doing." She untangled herself, swayed around, addressing no one in particular and continued, "Jane was a wonderful person, she was really clever, she spoke great English." Um; not hard, when in Greece . . . !

Then waving, swaying and pointing the index finger of her right hand she declared, "she was zee best foucking English teacher in Syros!"

Jane's daughter and I looked at each other, realising we were getting nowhere fast, so she thanked everyone for coming and supporting us and said, "Now, as my Mother would have said, let's all go to the pub."

Whoosh! Only immediate family and a couple of friends remained.

It was over: a couple of Greek women in black appeared, carrying trays of candied cakes and sweets, gesticulating that we should take them. Another ritual: the "professional mourners" of the town offer sustenance to the bereaved. We thanked them and exchanged pleasantries in sign language. Before leaving I stood at the foot of the grave, my shadow shading the already-wilting flowers, and thought, *what about a stone and epitaph?*

I smiled: *Here lies Meessis Yane, zee best foucking English teacher in Syros.*

Three Craws

Ron Thomas

Three craws sat upon a wa',
sat upon a wa', sat upon a wa',
three craws sat upon a wa'
on a cold and frosty morning

There they were, the Crowe brothers, sitting with their parents in the café, chatting to each other as if they didn't have a care in the world.

I knew better.

I had awoken that morning, a year ago, and felt magic in the air. It wasn't a clawing air: it was more an air of really intense expectation in my mind that something magical was about to happen.

And by the end of that day I was not disappointed.

They had hounded me ever since nursery just because I was different to them. Not because I was a girl but because I was born with Down's syndrome. No matter how many times they were told by their parents and teachers to stop, they continued to laugh and tease me in the nursery, playground, and in the street – whenever they saw me.

I didn't have feelings of humiliation or degradation. It was more like a lack of respect for who I am, which I got from almost everyone who knew me. Yes, respect is all I wanted from them but they couldn't or wouldn't see that.

The first craw couldnae flee at a',
he couldnae flee at a', he couldnae flee at a',
the first craw couldnae flee at a'
on a cold and frosty morning

Mr Crowe had built them a tree house in their back garden during the summer, and later that fateful day twelve year old Jack Crowe decided to climb the rope ladder up to it with the intention of having a clear out of all the rubbish which had accumulated over the summer. He had just got most of it out when he turned to hear his brother, Mike, shout something up to him. He slipped on a piece of ice at the edge of the house. Not being blessed with a set of wings he fell headlong to the hard ground.

His parents – along with Mike – took Jack to A&E were he was found to have broken both an arm and a leg. He was kept in overnight and next day transferred to the children's ward with both wrapped in plaster.

Two craws sat upon a wa',
sat upon a wa', sat upon a wa',
two craws sat upon a wa',
on a cold and frosty morning

The second craw couldnae find its ma,
couldnae find its ma, couldnae find its ma,
the second craw couldnae find its ma
on a cold and frosty morning

Eight year old Eric Crowe had been out with his friends when the incident with Jack had happened, so returned home to an empty house. Because of the panic which had ensued after Jack's fall, both parents had forgotten that Eric was not at home.

He was cold, so decided to make himself a coffee using the espresso machine. Although he had never used it before he had watched his mum and dad use it many times and felt confident enough to complete the task himself. During the proceedings he put the electric kettle on to upgrade the espresso to an Americano.

The espresso was completed without incident, but the upgrade was a different matter. He succeeded in transferring the coffee into a larger cup, but when he tried to pour the hot water into it the cup became too heavy for him to hold and he dropped it, leaving the hot water to pour out of the kettle on to his arms and legs.

Luckily a neighbour, who was in her garden, heard his screams. Upon seeing the situation in which Eric had put himself she rushed him into the bathroom, stood him in the bath, took his clothes off, turned on the shower and virtually hosed him down. Eventually the screaming subsided to a loud whimper so she wrapped him in a towel and drove him to A&E where they met his mother and father – who were waiting in reception for the doctor to tell them about Jack.

Each parent blamed each other for not thinking about Eric being out with his friends, or that one of them should have stayed at home to look after him when he came home.

Eric was examined, and because of his age they decided to keep him in overnight beside Jack.

One craw sat upon a wa',
sat upon a wa', sat upon a wa',
one craw sat upon a wa'
on a cold and frosty morning

The third craw fell and broke his jaw,
fell and broke his jaw, fell and broke his jaw,
the third craw fell and broke its jaw
on a cold and frosty morning

Mike and his parents eventually arrived home after a day of traumatic events and, after a light meal, Mike was sent to bed. Being the youngest of the family, six years old, he always had the lower of the bunk beds. As he was on his own for the first time he decided to try the upper bunk for a change, just to see what the view over the bedroom was like from Eric's angle. After five minutes he fell asleep.

In the middle of the night, not unexpectedly, he needed to go to the toilet. Completely forgetting that he was on the upper bunk he just stepped out the bed and crashed to the floor. The inevitable scream was heard by his parents who rushed into the bedroom to find Mike lying in agony.

For the second time that day they took the trip to A&E to find out that Mike had a broken jaw. Needless to say he too was kept in, but for a good bit longer than overnight.

With all three boys now in hospital, concerns were being raised about Mr & Mrs Crowe's parenting skills, and so, the next day the cases were referred to Social Services.

Nae craws sat upon a wa',
sat upon a wa', sat upon a wa',
nae craws sat upon a wa'
on that cold and frosty morning

Next day dawned and that air of magic which had surrounded me the previous day had disappeared and was, instead, replaced by an air of hope.

During the day the story of the three Crowe boys circulated the neighbourhood, and instead of feeling a sense of 'well they got what they deserved', I felt the need to visit them in hospital. Later that day, my mum and I went to the children's ward and we spoke to each one of them, wishing that they would soon be well – giving them the respect they didn't give to me.

Looking back, it may or may not have been an air of magic that day – but whatever it was, to me it was life changing. Because since then, we have all been firm friends and they have defended me against all who laugh and tease me.

Convict Girls

Brenda Thomson

Fear is trapped in the minds of girls
sentenced to sail beyond the seas.
Shackled, they sit
on the prison deck,
waiting for the clawing, eerie, fog
that hovers over the River Thames,
holding the ship captive, to lift.
The convicts, unwelcome in their homeland,
are not at one with any country.
A girl weeps, others follow.
Only emotion escapes.

The Greatest Stories

Luke Townsley

I once heard someone say that the greatest stories ever told are the ones that we have lived ourselves. I never gave it much thought until now – I guess my greatest story so far was three years ago.

That was when I and my three cousins Joel, Trevor and Nathan decided to have an adventure.

I was the youngest at 12 and I loved having fun with my older cousins, wandering and hunting was a good pastime. Trevor was the oldest at 14, he was the most adventurous of the gang and he was always up for anything – he was a little crazy but he was a good laugh. Joel was only a few months younger than him – he was an adventurous one as well. Most of our adventures started with him finding or doing something. He and Trevor were inseparable, wherever one went the other was sure to follow. Nathan was only slightly older than me at 13. He was the strongest of us and was also fast – him and Trevor were brothers but the argued more than anyone I knew – hell, they still do.

We were down in England for the summer, our trailers all in a row down the legendary lane of Old Weston – a massive oak stood strong to the left in between the two fields that made it hard for anyone else to see us – sometimes it was corn, sometimes sunflowers. It was different every few years.

This was our camp and we felt just as proud of it as we do our country.

It was at this camp that it all began for me. Most of my earliest memories are of that old lane, walking with my father down its winding paths, hunting for some rabbits or hares and sitting around the fire, sharing stories, singing songs and just enjoying everything.

Our adventure begins underneath the old oak, an oak that generations of my family have stayed around. Even at this age I know that my children will be brought to this oak.

Me and the gang sat around the tree sharing jokes and comparing our latest works of craftsmanship, whether it was bows, spears or slingshots – then we would go hunting to test them out.

"So what do you guys wanna do today?" It was a question that one of us was bound to ask at least once a day because some summer days can get long and boring. It was Trevor who had asked that day.

"I dunno, I think mam said she was goin' to the shop later, I might be busy with that," I said, whilst peeling a stick that would have made a brilliant spear. My father had given me a small pocket knife a few months before so I could make my own bows, spears and slingshots. I still have it today.

"Nah Luke, c'mon we gotta do something, look at the kind of day it is," Trevor said, whilst spreading his arms wide into the sunshine beaming down on us.

"We could go hunting?" Nathan suggested, as he attempted to climb the oak.

"I can't, my bow broke and this spear won't be ready for a while," I said. Trevor grabbed the stick and threw it deep into the field where Joel had gone wandering.

"C'mon man, think, you're the thinker," Trevor joked, as he gave me a mock slap across the cheek. He laughed, and I pushed him away. I turned around and see Joel running from the field of corn like it was about to blow, he had a huge grin on his face.

"Guys . . ." Joel stopped to catch his breath. ". . . I have found the most awesome thing ever, it is gonna blow your minds, you have to come see this!" I felt slightly reluctant so I inquired:

"What is it and how far?" I was worried what my parents would do if I just disappeared for a few hours – they got worried easily back then.

"C'mon Luke, don't be a pussy, just hurry up will ya?" Joel said as he started walking back into the field. Me, Trevor and Nathan followed hastily into the thick corn field.

We always carried some basic equipment with us whenever we adventured: a pocket knife, flint and steel or lighter, and some rope or string – the older boys had phones so I needed to use theirs to make calls.

We walked for about half an hour through the boiling hot field, all of us trying to keep quiet so the farmer wouldn't hear us. We had heard stories about traveller boys getting shot by farmers who found them snooping in their farms and fields.

We eventually reached our destination, right on the farmer's land. In the clearing we could see his house and all of his farm tools, but when we saw what Joel had found, we almost did backflips.

A massive green Tractor.

With the keys still in the ignition.

You can already guess yourself what happened: we leaped on to the thing. Joel was already in the driver's seat when we got there, and he knew how to drive a van so he was the most qualified of us. We all climbed on to relatively safe spots on the Tractor: I took the step just above the tow-bar, Trevor took the step next to the driver's seat and Nathan took the wheel arch. He held on to the seat that Joel was on.

"You ready, guys?!" Joel exclaimed as he turned the keys. The engine rumbled into life with some smoke, then burst forward with some speed behind it. We smashed clean through the farmer's brown picket fence and tore through the corn field at the highest speed the tractor would take us. We laughed and shouted loudly at our mischief – I looked back and saw the farmer running behind us, shouting and shaking his fist in the air. Then he turned and started running back to his house.

We tore down some more of the corn before we all leaped from the Tractor and ran like hell in the first direction that came to mind, laughing all the while. We ran for a few minutes, but we were scared paralysed when we heard the one sound every traveller boy fears most: the blast of a farmer's shotgun.

Then we were running in terror as fast as we could. Nathan tripped and I helped him up. Another shotgun blast, and I tripped over in fear. I got up quickly and ran behind the rest of the boys. We reached another picket fence and I tripped over it and scraped my elbows. We were in a large clearing with a barn in the middle – I could see the boys banging on the door trying to open it.

"Quick, under there!" I shouted, whilst pointing at a gap under the barn. I helped the boys through, but just as I was about to climb through I looked back and saw the farmer enter the clearing with a double-barrelled shotgun in hand. He reloaded as he saw me. Nathan helped me through the gap just as I heard another loud bang from the shotgun – the next thing I knew the gap I had just crawled through was blasted with shrapnel. If I had been any slower I would have been dead.

The boys ran to the other end of the barn and hid. Joel hid in a skip, Trevor hid in a barrel and Nathan hid behind a spool of copper. I ran to the first thing I could find, which happened to be a steel beam that was part of the main structure of the barn. I hid behind it as I heard footsteps just outside the barn door. I peeked, and saw a shadow from the gap beneath the door.

BOOM!!

And the door was blasted open in a spray of splinters and shrapnel. I hid my face from the blast behind the steel beam: my ears rang and I was utterly petrified, I honestly thought that this was the end of me – me and the boys in a barn with a psycho farmer.

"I know yer in here ya pricks, show yerselves slowly and I won't have to bury ya under this barn," the farmer said, before firing another shot into the barn. Everything lit up for a second and I heard him begin to reload.

Now I wasn't the bravest boy in the world and I will admit that, but on that day, I used my instincts, and although you may not believe this, this is what happened next.

I ran from behind the steel beam and before the farmer was even able to put one shell into the shotgun. My sharp right hook to the jaw sent him straight to the ground, and his shotgun clattered away into the barn.

"Eeh Aye, Eeh Aye, no bitch!" I shouted, as the farmer tried to stand and I kicked him in the nose, knocking his bloody face into the dirt. I thought about hitting him again but he was out cold. I left the shotgun as I ran down to the back of the barn – then Nathan did the funniest thing I have ever seen.

He stood and rammed through the weakened wood at the back of the barn, leaving a Nathan-shaped hole like one of those old cartoons. We wasted no time in following behind him – we ran straight back into the field, and ran till our lungs felt like they were filled with the fires of oblivion. About two minutes later I heard another bang from the shotgun.

"FUCKING GYPSIES!!" I heard the farmer shout, way behind us, as I reached a wall. I had a huge smile on my face due to the fact that behind this wall was the road that led home. I was on my own at that moment – was every man for himself and we knew it, so I climbed the wall as fast as I could and fell face-first at the other side.

Everything went blank.

I awoke about ten minutes later with a slap from Trevor; he let out a large sigh of relief as I opened my eyes and sat up whilst rubbing my head. We were back at the old lane – not at the trailers of course – but we were all back safely.

"Joel carried you back here, we thought you were dead at first man, you gave us a scare." Trevor said, as he helped me up. I wobbled for a second but a few steps later we were walking back to the trailers. We all shared our version of events whilst laughing and cheering like knights who had just slayed a dragon.

". . . And you, Luke, you came out of nowhere then bam!" Nathan exclaimed, whilst shadow boxing. We laughed and joked some more before Trevor exclaimed loudly, "that was Legendary!!"

"I wouldn't say it was legendary . . ." I said with a smirk. "But it would make the greatest story."

Message in a Bottle

Anne Whittet

April 2015

Dear Flora,

You will never read this letter, it will never be posted, we have never met and the question will never be answered. If you could read this letter you would know who I am, but I don't know your address or whether you are still alive. You have teased my imagination.

My mother, Grace, is your cousin. You were great friends. Grace is in her eighties now and she has spoken of you on many occasions, always with great fondness. I have heard tales of your youth from her and seen photographs of you together. There is one in particular of you and my mother. In black and white, it was taken when you were young girls. You are standing arm in arm beneath a tree – it would have been taken in summer, and the tree is in full leaf. In this photo you are both laughing at some shared joke. You are wearing beautiful nineteen forties summer dresses. Yours, Flora, was a knee length gingham check, belted at the waist in the same fabric. Tied round your dark wavy hair is a matching scarf. My mother wore a dress with a Peter Pan collar, buttons up the front, in a print of seashells, it was stunning. I would love to wear those! You are two carefree, very pretty young women, although my mother, Grace, always said that you were more than just pretty. A wee concession, but I can tell from the old photo that she was right.

So I know a bit about you Flora, having heard snippets. I have heard, too, about the large house in Reston in the Borders where you lived with your parents and sisters. It was haunted, and my mother told me what took place there and how your family reluctantly decided to move out. That, though is another story (one which I have written about elsewhere in detail)!

I have asked my mother if this episode in the lovely house in Reston – and having to leave it – was what prompted your emigration to Canada. Her memory is foggy now so she can't be sure. Were you simply lured like so many others to that wonderful country? I wish I had asked her this question at a time when she may have remembered. Your older sister Rachel did not go to Canada with you. By that time she was married and, having two small children, was too settled here to uproot her family. I knew her well in my childhood. You and Grace lost touch over the years – these things happen. There was no sadness about it, and fond memories cannot be tarnished. To me, you are the laughing beauty beneath the tree standing with my mother. You – or who you became – are the question which will remain unanswered, not least because you will never read this.

For sentiment or fun, I shall put this letter into a quaint old blue bottle and cast it into the sea. I like this idea, it somehow fits the enigmatic picture I have of you. It will add to my flimsy perception of you: one based on small, happy stories of times you shared with Grace, and that photo of you two in another life, a carefree moment frozen in time under the boughs of a silver birch, my favourite tree. I like to think the tree remains to this day.

The message in the bottle will bob away from me, to who knows where? I shall watch till it is out of sight. I will daydream about the slimmest, most remote chance of it ever being found by another human being. It is a small ritual, romantic even. It adds substance to the mystery of you. That is why, in my daydream, I will imagine it found and picked up, perhaps by a small child, whose parent will remove it from plump four-year-old fingers and find inside this wistful letter, gently smile, and go off with a feeling of intrigue, and the story of the blue bottle his child found washed up by the tide.

A Kelly, Grace's daughter

Moving On

Isla Whittington

Anger. Rage. Adrenaline flooding out of the pancreas, washing away all sense or reason. Cheek twitches. Jaw muscles spasming, clenching down hard. Each breath is heavy with emotion. Unstoppable. Uncontrollable. Nonsensical.

Breathe, she thought to herself. *This is not the time.* There would be time later to be angry. Time to vent. Time to scream. But now was not it. She had to keep her wits about her if she was to get this sorted.

The morning had started off much the same as every other morning. Alarm; shower; morning coffee. And the paper. Headline had been the typical gore, terror and death, and she had flicked through the pages barely reading the words, staring listlessly at the pictures and wondering what the world had come to. It was a sad when journalists only ever found a thrill in death and gore. Surely there had to be some good out there in the world. Seriously, was this all we were capable of?

A small ad at the bottom of page twelve caught her attention. "Two bedroom cottage in quaint setting with sizeable garden . . ." And the picture. A picture of her house. Her home. Her place of existence for the last nine months. *The bitch! She's selling it out from underneath me!* Well technically not from underneath, since Terry hadn't been staying there for the past few weeks, but putting technicalities aside, it was Terry's home. She had chosen it. Viewed it. Mortgaged it. Bought it. So the papers were in The Bitch's name – but it was not as though she helped to pay for it, it had only been arranged that way so that The Bitch could get permanent residency. *Pah!*

The Bitch: aka Jane Armitage; sometimes referred to as Terry's better half, although Terry had long ago decided that those who thought of Jane as the better half clearly did not know Jane. Jane was American. Not that that bothered Terry, she had nothing against Americans for the most part. Their accents could be grating and their attitude often arrogant, but generally all the Americans Terry had met were decent, down to earth people. She had once even believed the same of Jane. Well, not now! Definitely not now!

Slamming her half-drained mug down in the sink, Terry grabbed her bag and march off down to the local estate agents. It was a twenty minute stroll, which she managed to reduce to a five-minute, fuming march. Barging through the front doors, almost knocking them off their hinges – and almost leaving the little old lady behind them on the floor – Terry stormed up to the desk. She took no heed of the queue patiently waiting, and demanded to see Mr Randel immediately.

The secretary behind the desk looked at Terry with what she'd obviously hoped would be the most scathing look ever experienced. In fact it came out more like a confused stare, but either way it had little effect on the livid, partially-frothing Terry. The secretary, Ms Johnson, was in a particularly great mood as it happened, and there was no way she was letting a tall, short-haired, feminine attempt at masculinity ruin her good mood.

"There's a queue." Ms Johnson pointed out.

"Screw the queue."

Ms Johnson's mouth dropped a few inches.

"Mr Randel! Now, if you don't mind!" Terry demanded, before Ms Johnson had time to argue. A very taken aback Ms Johnson continued to stare with a look that was meant to say *fat chance, pal*, but came out more like ". . ."

"Has the colour of your hair gone to your brain or are you actually able to compute what I'm saying?" Terry snapped, irritated by the contemptuous looks and lack of action. Shrugging, Terry leaned over the counter, grabbed the phone and rapped on the button labeled *Mr Randel's office*. It was written in child-like handwriting that may well have belonged to the bottle-blonde Ms Johnson, but Terry was inclined to think that monkeys were unable to write.

There was a pause in which the whole queue and the security staff, plus a very baffled Ms Johnson, whose jaw had finally hit the floor, stared at Terry.

"Yes, Mr Randel, which office are you in? Uh huh!"

The phone clicked back on to the receiver. Terry glanced at the spectators, handed a tissue to Ms Johnson – "you're dribbling" – and marched off to the elevators.

As the elevator ascended and the floor numbers ticked past Terry thought back to when she had first set eyes on Jane in that quiet, infrequently-packed pub on one of Aberdeen's many subsidiary streets. There she had been, sitting in the corner, cuddling a large whiskey, her eyes focused on a place somewhere above the door with an oddly detached and almost haunted look on her face. She had been the only person in the bar which, considering it was noon on a Monday, was not surprising. Terry instantly liked her good looks, the sharp features, well toned body and long brown hair pulled back into a tight plait disappearing down her back – but what caught Terry's attention the most were the torn and mud stained clothes that clung to Jane's powerful frame.

Terry was a successful recruitment consultant, spending much of her time in the city or on the road. She had always lived alone, preferring the solitary lifestyle and the freedom that it offered her over and above the closeness of a relationship. It wasn't that she didn't date. Sure she dated. Mostly for a few weeks before her latest catch began the typical "shall we move in?" act, toothbrush turning up in the bathroom with the classic lesbian script for partnership spilling out of their mouths on a daily basis. It wasn't for her. It was too intense and far too independence-limiting. Or so she thought, until Jane had turned up. Jane was different. She had shown no desire to have anything long term, and as the days turned to months Terry actually found herself falling in love. A surreal experience in itself, but one she would happily re-experience.

The lift doors opened. Terry stepped out onto the sixth floor, the corridor stretching away on either side. Turning right, she stormed down the hallway, head flicking from side to side, checking room numbers until she came to room 615. Thrusting the door open she began to protest in the strongest terms.

"Mr Randel, you have no . . ." Her voice died away as the room hit her.

The bucktoothed, mousey Mr Randel was sitting behind his desk, sweat streaming down his face, soaking into his collar. In front of him, casually folded into one of the low armchairs was the tall frame of Jane.

"You bitch!" yelped Terry.

"Nice of you to join us Terry. Care to take a seat?" Jane waved at the adjacent arm chair with a rather slick-looking gun, her eyes never leaving the dripping face of Mr Randel. "I was just explaining a few things to Mr Randel here. It turns out he doesn't understand the concept of not embezzling his clients' money."

"Well, as much as that is wrong, I would encourage him to take as much money from you as he desires," snarled Terry.

"Oh really, Terry! Stop getting your knickers in a wad!"

"I'll do precisely what I want with my knickers. You're selling my bloody house! You cow!"

"No, I'm not. I needed a way in, that's all." The gun was waved in the general direction of Mr Randel. "I needed to talk to this little prick. Turns out there are people who don't like what he's doing. You can have the house back. I'll take it off the market after this."

"What's with the gun?" queried Terry, slightly mollified.

"Certain people want things to change. Permanently!"

"You're going to kill him?" Terry's skin was turning glacial in shock. She knew Jane was capable of hurting people (that much was clear from recent events), but a bullet to the head was either going a step too far – or was the American way of dealing with things.

"You can't just shoot someone because someone else doesn't like what they are doing, Jane!"

"Sure you can!"

Terry stared at Jane, heart pounding. As much as she hated Jane right now for trying to sell the house, this wasn't right. This wasn't right! "Please, Jane."

Jane continued to stare at Mr Randel and his sweat-stained clothing. Her disgust was evident, but lurking underneath was a slight hesitation. Something in Terry's voice was making her think.

"Terry, you'd better wait outside."

"Jane, please don't!"

"Outside, Terry!"

Terrified Terry inched backwards out the door, pulling it closed quietly. Anger had transformed into fear and disbelief. A sinking feeling. That unmistakeable wobble in the gut. Blinking back tears of horror, Terry stood and stared at the closed office door. Silence stretched to the point of bursting.

Turning away, tears leaking from the emotional dam, Terry ran back towards the lift, hands over her ears. *How could she?! How could she?!* The tears were running freely. Time slowed. The lift dawdled on its decent. The tears spilled out of her broken heart and down her cheeks. *How could she?!* Jane wasn't a killer. Not the Jane she knew. The lift touched down. The doors opened. A red-eyed Terry dashed out the building, the reception staring after her.

Things had been fractious between her and Jane for months, eventually reaching a climax a few weeks ago when, after several smashed vases, Terry had stormed out. The hope that time and patience would right the situation had faded as the weeks passed. She had tried several times to get hold of Jane, but the robotic O2 voicemail was her only reward. Now she was faced with the terrible thought that the woman she had loved – and indeed still did love – was a killer. That was simply unforgivable in her book. There could be no reconciliation now. It was time for Terry to move on.

About the Editor . . .

Claire Askew is a poet and writer based in Edinburgh. Her debut poetry collection, 'This changes things,' was shortlisted for the inaugural Edwin Morgan Poetry Award in 2014, and published by Bloodaxe Books in 2016. Her debut novel-in-progress, *Three Rivers*, won the 2016 Lucy Cavendish Fiction Prize, and is represented by Peters Fraser & Dunlop Associates. Claire holds a PhD in Creative Writing and Contemporary Women's Poetry from the University of Edinburgh, and is also the editor of *Starry Rhymes: 85 Years of Allen Ginsberg* (Read This Press, 2011) and a new anthology of contemporary poetry about Edinburgh, forthcoming in autumn 2016 from Freight Books.

. . . and the Contributors

Dianne Alexander was born in Fordyce. She has made her way slowly round Scotland, living in many villages and towns until, she is hoping finally, settling in Rosewell. She caught the writing bug shortly after holidaying in Seville; teased by a book she was reading which took place there. She wondered how easy or hard it would be to write her own novel. That mystery is still unraveling.

Mark Bateman has always wanted to write a novel but could never find the time and ironically it took his wife's illness to provide it. She had to retire because of her health in 2010 and Mark gave up work to look after her. He toyed around with a few ideas for a while before starting his first novel properly at the end October 2013 when his wife had a spell in hospital. He completed his first draft in early March 2015. Looking for some positive critique he joined Tyne & Esk later that year and the Haddington group has helped him immensely. He is now working to finish his novel, a crime story, and already has started on the draft of a second.

Margaret Beck attends the Musselburgh Tyne & Esk Writers group.

Stella Hervey Birrell writes short stories, novels and poems, mostly for and about women. Her debut novel, *How Many Wrongs Make A Mr Right?* was published by Crooked Cat Books in 2016. She is a regular member of the Dalkeith Tyne & Esk Writers group. Stella lives in the rural idyll of Pencaitland, East Lothian, with her cat, husband and children. In that order.

Stuart Blair lives in Bonnyrigg.

Rita Bradd, published since 2007 in print and online anthologies, was long-listed for the Herald/McCash prize with *The Herrin Trail*, now a Filmpoem; featured on BBC Scotland's Culture Studio; appears in several publications including a Sma Buik by Poems-for-All at StAnza 2016, where film *City of Adelaide Bleeds* featuring Kevin Cadwallender was an installation. Rita appeared on BBC 3's The Verb duetting with Ira Lightman; and Book Week Scotland 2015. Her first pamphlet by Red Squirrel is due in 2017. She has published a series of 'The Three Craws' scripts in Scots/English, and is completing writing her book. www.ritabradd.com

Andy Broadfoot says he finds writing about himself in the third person something of a challenge, even though he is often a character in his own work. He's hell bent on making sense of lived experiences by probing the boundaries between memory and imagination, picking at the seams. For this reason, he can't decide between writing fiction and narrative non-fiction and so chooses to do both. He claims to be exploring, challenging and re-interpreting accepted truths, hoping the people in his stories will come to terms with their flaws as human beings.

Elspeth Brown is a member of Dunbar Writers and enjoys the chance to share writing experiences. She finds the countryside of East Lothian inspiring, especially when walking her dog. She has had several pamphlets published and two books of poetry: *A Crab in the Moon's Mouth,* and *Skunk Cabbage*. Her poetry and short stories have been in *Southlight, Markings, Gutter, Poetry Scotland,* and *London Magazine,* among others. She has had a play about James Clerk Maxwell performed in the Edinburgh Fringe and Science Festival. Other writing interests include John Muir, and Black Agnes, who was as persistent as Madge Elliot.

Ford Bull is a generic millennial from Mayfield. Find him on Instagram at BAKE_N_SKATE_91

After trying her hand at most things, **Julia M Carman** now concentrates on flash fiction, which she sometimes tries to pass off as poetry. Joining Tyne & Esk Writers has improved her writing, although she still struggles to finish a story.

Creative and adventure-loving, **Moira Cormack** belongs to Tyne & Esk Writers in Dalkeith, and Bagatelle, a local Storytelling group. Since going on a creative writing holiday she has been compelled to write, dashing out sentences between peeling and mashing the spuds. Everything around Moira creeps into her writing. She walks her dog beside the river, unravelling plots with each step. Moira has never outgrown her love of fairy tales and has a special fondness for witches. Her first novel for children, *The Witch of Land and Sea*, is published in July of 2016.

Yvonne Dalziel has written unfinished stories and half finished dramas for years but only started finishing things when she joined Tyne & Esk Writers. She was their Writer of the Year in 2014, won the Glasgow Women's Library Bold Types prize in 2015 and Jupiter Artland prize in 2016. Has finished her first novel, *The Gift of Strangers,* and hopes eventually to complete a radio play and have it broadcast.

Michael Davenport was born and brought up in Eyemouth, Berwickshire. Before retirement in 2001 he taught Science in East Lothian secondary schools. His interests include scuba diving and geology. Poetry booklets *Fish Alive* (2006), *Tell me About Them* (2009) and *The Science of Lives* (2014) were published by Tyne & Esk Writers. In 2006 he won the Tyne & Esk Writer of the Year competition.

Pat Dickson was born in Dundee in 1946, has also lived in Ayr, Dunbar, and Duns, and spent 14 years in south west France. She returned to Scotland three years ago after her husband died, and settled in North Berwick. Pat loves being a member of the North Berwick writing group, and writes mostly short stories, though she has a book about life in France on the go. Pat's other interests include reading (voraciously), walking her dog on the glorious local beaches, volunteering at Day Centre, keeping up with friends, and helping out with two tiny grandchildren. She has no literary ambitions whatsoever, she just enjoys writing.

Since joining North Berwick Writers, **Lorna Dixon** has been working on developing her skill at short story writing. Previously she had written, acted in and directed plays on the Edinburgh Festival Fringe and since moving to North Berwick has written and directed plays about the North Berwick Witch trials and Robert Louis Stevenson's local connections. Lorna is currently investigating the activities of suffragettes in the area with a view to creating a dramatic piece about the lead up to the burning of St Mary's Whitekirk.

Ian Donaldson is 58 years old and was born and bred in Port Seton from long-standing fishing stock on both sides of his family. Ian says: "Where once almost my entire family had working connections with the sea, only my brother Adam still retains these traditions as a fishmonger – not as a fisherman, which would have been the case in the past." Ian has written for various articles and occasions, including weekly match reports for Musselburgh Rugby Club, poems, and after-dinner speeches. He attends Port Seton Writers Club.

Paul Duffney, a retired technician, thinks best when he is writing and hopes that the power of our words to create new realities is one of the best bets for the human race in the future. If we don't like the world as it is, we can write it as it should be.

Victoria Fletcher – Vicky – was born in Edinburgh in 1942. She went to school at a convent in Essex, then spent a year at the Duns High School in Berwickshire. She attended the Prince of Wales School of Physiotherapy and qualified in 1964. She worked mainly in Edinburgh. Vicky retired on health grounds in 1989, and did a ScotVec course at Telford College in Librarianship and Information Studies. She moved to Haddington and started to write poetry, having her first poem published in 1993. Since then she has also written a book about her early childhood, and now a sequel to it.

Moira Galbraith attends the Haddington Tyne & Esk Writers group.

Kenny Gilchrist has been a Dalkeith member of Tyne & Esk Writers for many years. He has had some poems published in previous Tyne & Esk anthologies. Kenny has recited at the Lennoxlove Book Festival, and has had a short story published in *A Sense of Place*. Kenny enjoys reading other poets especially poems by Edwin Morgan. Scottish friction. Scottish fiction.

Ruth Gilchrist spent her childhood in East Africa, her teenage years on The Isle of Wight and has lived and worked in Kent and The Lake District. Currently settled beside the lovely Bilsdean she combines a love of poetry with the trials of raising boys, restoring an old cottage and negotiating with nature to create a garden. She has had work published in various local anthologies, can be heard reading her work at numerous local events and is the current Tyne & Esk Writer of the Year.

Billy Graham was the winner of the Tyne & Esk Writer of the Year Award in 2012. He is the author of several books, most recently *Charlie's Gold* (2016). He attends the Haddington Tyne & Esk Writers group.

Jamie Graham is a copywriter, author and poet from East Lothian. His passion for writing began at an early age when he won a BBC Radio competition for his story 'Jack the Bucket Man'. His biggest writing challenge to date was penning 24 kids stories in 24 hours to raise money for charity. He has also written a novel based in Edinburgh called *The Price of a Pint*.

Cathie Gray attends the Haddington Tyne & Esk Writers group.

Penny Hext lives and writes in Edinburgh, close to the Pentland Hills. She is currently working on a novel.

Frances Hider writes creative non-fiction with a special interest in the relationship between humans and animals and what this tells us about ourselves. Her writing has recently featured in the University of Edinburgh, Institute for Advanced Studies in the Humanities 'Dangerous Women Project'. Frances gained an Open University Diploma in Creative Writing, followed by an MA in Creative Writing at Edinburgh Napier University. Frances lives in Penicuik and is currently writing a book about how dogs influence and change our lives.

Jim Inglis says: "[the piece excerpted in this anthology] is my first attempt at writing a novel and I am thoroughly enjoying it. I am 72, have been married 48 years, with three sons. My biggest challenge has been learning the computer, especially Microsoft Word, which I didn't even have on my computer to start with!"

Gordon Jamieson attends the Port Seton Tyne & Esk Writers group.

When **Mary Johnston** retired, she had time available to pursue her interest and talent for writing. Since 1997 the writing support available in Dalkeith has provided her with valuable encouragement and constructive criticism.

Using the writing group and Creative Writing Fellow as sounding boards, critical friends and inspiration, Mary has had many have poems and short stories published in various Scottish magazines, has self-published six collections of poetry and a collection of short stories. Mary says, "as an older, retired person in Midlothian, the writing group do not only help and support me creatively, they have saved me from gardening and lunching out too much. I cannot overstate how significant a role they play in my week and my life."

Anne Jones is Scottish; wee with a big mouth.

For the (approximately) one-third of his life spent in Europe, **Jeff Kemp** has lived in East Lothian, where he has been part of the Musselburgh Writers group for several years (having begun the habit of writing in the previous third of his life, which was mostly spent in Asia). Jeff enjoys exploring the liminal space that writing a poem allows, letting rhythm frame how ideas emerge while holding lightly to an initial sense of something that, with luck, magic, or grace, may come to fill a page. It's addictive but it isn't illegal and doesn't make him fat, so he guesses he'll do it again.

After a career mostly within the sphere of Design – as a practitioner and as a lecturer in Design History – **Graham Leake** joined the Dalkeith group of Tyne & Esk Writers in 2002 after his retirement. His writing is mostly prose with an element, he hopes, of humour. He published a collection, *The Road to California,* through Tyne & Esk Writers in 2013.

For many years, **Elsie Lindsay** was a member of The Byre Writers in St Andrews where the group concentrated on playwrighting. When she moved to North Berwick in September 2015, she was delighted to see a notice in the library with information about the local Tyne & Esk Writers and immediately became a member. Since joining, she has enjoyed exploring ideas suggested by the "prompts" and has found writing short stories more satisfying and less frustrating than trying to construct a drama for the stage. She also appreciates the support and back-up within the Tyne & Esk organisation.

Lyn Livingstone has been a member of the Musselburgh writing group for more than 20 years. She writes poetry mainly and occasionally short stories, but has never had anything published apart from items in Tyne & Esk anthologies published by previous writing fellows. Lyn enjoys reading her poems at the group and listening to the work of others.

Bruce Lumsden is a retired Wildlife Surveyor, who moved with his family to live in East Lothian nearly ten years ago. He writes, paints and sculpts, often inspired by the local coast and countryside with its rich scenery and wildlife. There is a novel in the making, but meantime he concentrates on short stories, often utilising dialogue with quirky, off-beat, and sometimes numerous styles, drawing on his wealth of experience. Bruce's works juxtapose real characters with imaginary situations, or vice versa. This allows his experiences to be brought to bear without causing embarrassment to some of the characters!

Neil McGowan is a prolific author of dark fiction – including horror novels *The Surgeon*, *Nanobite*, novella *The Loch*, and the collected short stories *Don't Drink the Water* – as well as several stories that have been published online and in magazines. He lives in Scotland and is a keen cyclist, taking inspiration from the landscape around him. He says writing is more fun than work and, he is nothing like the characters in his novels. Honest.

Rebecca McKinney was born in Colorado and raised in Northern California. She came to Edinburgh as a student in 1994 and never left. She is a mum, community development practitioner, ex-council worker, and slave to a small but demanding cat. She writes for love, therapy and a tiny bit of money. Her début novel *Blast Radius* was published by Sandstone Press in 2015.

Sarah McLean is 22 and a student at Glasgow University, studying English Literature and French. She knew she wanted to be an author since her poem was put up on the wall in primary six, and since then she has written two novels (which she is in the process of editing.) She has had two poems published in *The National Anthology Of Poetry* and *Between The Lines*, which she says is the greatest achievement of her life. "I realised something when I was ten and my teacher read out my poem to the class: I need to write."

LesleyMay Miller is an artist and poet. She is a member of 'Words on Canvas,' a group of writers in the National Galleries of Scotland. She combines her words and visual art in artistbooks, sculpture and soundscapes. Her poetry has been published in magazines such as *The Eildon Tree, The Rialto* and in anthologies. She created a sculpture garden in the Scottish Borders. She now draws inspiration from living by the coast.

After many holidays in East Lothian **Malky Mitchell** set up business in Dunbar and moved to North Berwick. His love of the area inspired him to begin a series of books, under the pseudonym Ethrick Brown (work it out), and based on the idea "Nothing ever happens in North Berwick." The first, subtitled *The Somali Pirate Adventure*, was well received and described as "laugh-out-loud nonsense which made perfect sense," with a well thought out plot and excellent characters. The sequel, subtitled *Judgement Day*, is work in progress. Malky joined Tyne & Esk in January 2016 and hasn't missed a week since.

Gordon Moodie was born and brought up in Edinburgh and has lived in Midlothian for over 40 years. He only started writing after he retired. He writes poems and short stories in both Scots and English and has had several pieces published in Lallans.

Shirley Muir has a degree in molecular biology from Edinburgh University. She was a technical writer and journalist in the pharmaceutical, computer and oil industries before retiring and embarking on a second career writing fiction. She now lives by the sea near Edinburgh, Scotland and she writes short fiction, poetry and memoir. She is particularly fond of science writing and is now writing science fiction stories. Shirley won the inaugural Crediton Short Story Competition in 2015 with 'Trapped' and took second prize in the Henshaw competition in June 2015 with 'Time to Flee'. Find out more at https://fidrawritings.wordpress.com

Jane Patmore works as a celebrant holding weddings and funerals and spends much of her working time writing and talking about other people's lives. Since joining Musselburgh Writers in spring 2015 Jane has been exploring writing in her own voice and creating fiction rather than fact. In Musselburgh Writers Jane has found a group of friends as well as inspiration and encouragement to experiment with all different types of work. The piece Jane wrote for this anthology was inspired by a topic suggested to the writing group by Creative Writing Fellow Claire Askew.

Eric Platten joined Tyne & Esk Writers in late 2014 when he left full time work. He is a member of the Penicuik group. Prior to the writing group the only things he had written were an attempt at a memoir – which he started in 2001/2 and hasn't done much with since – and a piece following the passing of his mother in 2008. He mainly writes poetry, based on what is in the news and what tickles his fancy when the creative urge hits him.

Jules A Riley (born 1943) is an Anglo-Belgian writer living in Musselburgh, Scotland. His short stories have been published in the UK, USA, Mexico & India. His first collection of previously published short stories, *The Man In The Sepia Photographs* was published in 2016 and is available through Amazon.

Keith Saunders was born and bred in North Wales. He was educated at Aberystwyth University after which he became first a teacher, and then a lecturer in Geography. He came to writing late and has completed one novel which he hopes to publish soon, as well as writing stories and poems which have appeared in various collections. He is married and has a son and two granddaughters.

After travelling extensively abroad and living in various locations in Britain, he and his wife decided to move to Dunbar to be close to the family, which they did – on Referendum Day!

Anne Shivas grew up in Edinburgh, and has since lived a third of her adult life in Israel, Vermont and the UK. Her poetry has been published in journals and anthologies in Israel, New Zealand, the USA and Scotland. She has an MFA in poetry from Drew University, NJ and her first collection *Whit Grace* will be published by Word Press (USA) in 2017.

Cheryl Smith's love of writing began early; her first memory is of making marks on paper and 'reading' them to her dolls. She studied philosophy, language, history and ethnology, and worked for many years as an adult educator, occasionally writing and having work published here and there. She has been blogging on health and wellbeing since 2010, and her first book, *Being Mrs Smith*, was due for publication by O Books in June 2016.

Cheryl lives in Roslin, where she loves walking in the glen with her dogs . . . unless it's raining, when she prefers a sofa, a good book and a purring cat. Sometimes she knuckles down to writing her second book.

Jock Stein's first involvement with the arts was as a pianist and piper, and later as chair of a Scottish Arts Charity, the Wayfarer Trust. At Carberry Tower he was responsible for an annual summer Family Arts Festival. He is also treasurer of the Creative Arts Retreat Movement. Since retirement he has been actively writing poetry, and enjoys being part of Tyne & Esk Writers.

Cynthia Stephens was born in Edinburgh and grew up in East Lothian. Much of her childhood was spent swimming in the sea and riding on horseback. Later she studied English and Spanish language and literature at the University of Newcastle upon Tyne, then went to live in Toledo, Spain, where she taught English. She has published articles about the writer Jorge Luis Borges. Having spent thirty years away she returned to Scotland, and currently works as a Spanish translator from her seaside home in Dunbar. She has not been on a horse for four decades.

From the ages of 3 to 11, **Diana Stevens** lived in Austria, and she has worked in London, Geneva and Edinburgh. Following a career in admin, two children, and a husband, the OU course Start Writing Fiction led to two Creative Writing modules with the OU and inspired her to join Tyne & Esk Writers, at the same time continuing with an OU Open Arts degree which paradoxically somewhat restricted creative writing. As well as attempting to write poetry, surprising herself, she also writes short stories, often sci-fi or apocalyptic.

Brought up in Inverness, **Judith Stewart** is still a Highlander at heart after over fifty years in lovely Haddington. She started writing about 20 years ago through the encouragement of her husband, who offered to buy her a word processor if she would use it to write stories. Three years later, she retired from work and joined the newly-formed Haddington Writers' Group. Gradually, the stories became shorter and shorter and eventually mutated into poetry, which is so wonderfully concise.

On retirement from being a Local Councillor in 2007, **Sheila Thacker** started writing down some of the many stories she had related to her family over the years. On joining the Penicuik Tyne & Esk Writers group, she gained confidence and began to write short stories – some based on life experience, and some purely fictional. 'Cultures clash and invent rituals' is based on a family event from 2000. Sheila has previously written 'Lost in grief' which was published in *Palm Trees in Midlothian* in 2010. Two other short stories have been printed in T&E magazine *Scrivens*.

Ron Thomas says: "While helping clients balance their books, I dream of a life of crime. Crime fiction, that is. Five years ago I published my first book and have now published my third, *The Austen Trinity*, a murder mystery, linked to the life of Jane Austen. I get a lot of job satisfaction from accountancy but I also wanted to do something creative in my spare time. I've always enjoyed books about crime so the next step was to write some myself. I also gain inspiration from television and newspaper stories but I add a twist that's entirely from my own imagination.

Brenda Thomson writes poetry and prose. Much of her poetry is written in Doric, the mither tongue of her parents. After she retired she visited the Immigration Museum in Melbourne, Australia, and became interested in the stories behind the convicts who were transported from Britain to Australia from the late 18th century until the middle of the 19th century. This interest has developed and she is now writing a novel about a fictional young Scottish convict who was transported beyond the seas.

Luke Townsley is 16 years old and has been writing for six years. He is currently unpublished but plans to be published within the next two to three years. He mostly writes Sci-Fi, Action and Horror, all based in the UK – because it is the perfect setting for all three, as there is so much history and beauty that makes it perfect.

Luke is currently based in Haddington in East Lothian and is a proud member of the Tyne & Esk Haddington Writers group.

Anne Whittet says: "I am so happy to be included in the anthology, and so grateful to Claire for including it. I joined Tyne & Esk over three years ago and feel this has channelled my interest in a positive way. I now have quite a collection of stories and other pieces on varying themes. I find writing an absorbing process and particularly enjoy the creative bit of mentally composing ideas, prior to committing them to the page. The challenge of fine tuning then follows. It is all immensely enjoyable."

Isla Whittington is 27 and has always been interested in writing. Working around her Open University degree in maths and physics, she finds that writing can be an excellent way to relax after a heavy dose of logical thought. After many faltering starts over the years she has finally found her feet and has in fact started something that could turn into a first novel.